Ordered, That this Order be a Standing O...
Johnson.)

Friday, 17th *January*

Ordered, That, notwithstanding the Order of the House of 18th November relating to nomination of Members of the Expenditure Committee, Mr. Tim Sainsbury be discharged from the Committee and Mr. Robert Adley be added to the Committee for the remainder of this Parliament.

Ordered, That this Order be a Standing Order of the House.—(*Mr. Walter Harrison*.)

The membership of the Defence and External Affairs Sub-Committee is as follows:—

Colonel Sir Harwood Harrison, (*Chairman*).	Mr. Geoffrey Finsberg.
	Mr. Anthony Kershaw.
Sir Frederic Bennett.	Dr. Maurice Miller.
Mr. James Boyden.	Mr. John Roper.
Mr. Bernard Co...	Mr. Neville Sandelson.

The cost of preparing for publication the Shorthand Minutes of Evidence taken before the Defence and External Affairs Sub-Committee was £56·41 in Session 1974 and £42·52 in Session 1974–75.

The cost of printing and publishing this Report is estimated by Her Majesty's Stationery Office at £1,528·50.

TABLE OF CONTENTS

NOTE

In the Report, references to the Minutes of Evidence are indicated by the letter " Q " followed by the number of the Question referred to. References to Memoranda included in the Minutes of Evidence are indicated by the word " Evidence " followed by the number of the page referred to. References to Memoranda included in the Appendices are indicated by the word " Appendix " followed by the number of the Appendix referred to.

FIRST REPORT

The Expenditure Committee have agreed to the following Report :—

CENTRAL MANAGEMENT OF THE SERVICES

INTRODUCTION

1. Since the establishment of the Expenditure Committee in 1971, it has become increasingly apparent to the Defence and External Affairs Sub-Committee that the three Services still enjoy a great degree of autonomy in their management and organisation. The Sub-Committee has examined Service training and the RAF manpower economy project, two subjects which illustrate the compartmentalised and single-Service approach prevailing within the Ministry of Defence. We set out below our assessment of these two inquiries and draw attention to the lack of co-ordination and direction provided in these areas by the Central Staffs of the Ministry of Defence.

SERVICE TRAINING

2. In paragraphs 34–36 of the Ninth Report of Session 1971–72[1] the Expenditure Committee recorded the results of their initial inquires into Service training. The main point of principle to emerge was the question of the extent to which training should be conducted on a tri-Service or joint Service basis. Training was, and still is, primarily the responsibility of the single Services, each of which has its own Director of Training, but a Defence Training Committee (DTC) exists to co-ordinate training where more than one Service is involved. The Chairman of the DTC had stated that his Committee started from the premise that single-Service training was absolutely right, but a start had been made on rationalising some relatively small items.

3. The Expenditure Committee of Session 1971–72 questioned this basic premise and considered that, while there might be very real obstacles to unified or joint Service training, single-Service identities were too often preserved unnecessarily. They thought there was more to be gained from encouraging a closer understanding at all levels of the work and problems of all three Services, and they noted that the DTC acted only on matters of an inter-Service nature referred to it by one of the Services. Accordingly, the Committee recommended that the DTC should actively seek out areas for co-operation in and co-ordination of training by the three Services, and should not wait until it was compelled to act.

4. In reply to this recommendation, the Ministry stated in February 1973 that the DTC would continue to seek out areas in which there might be advantages in rationalisation or inter-Service co-operation.[2] They added, however, that in the past few years the field had been so widely reviewed that the scope for further action of this kind was unlikely to be large.

---

[1] Ninth Report from the Expenditure Committee, Session 1971–72, H.C. (1971–72) 516—I.
[2] Cmnd. 5245.

5. Against this rather discouraging background, the Defence and External Affairs Sub-Committee of Session 1973–74 sought from the Ministry comparative statements of the Services' training costs for seven trades and a note on any unified training ventures undertaken. When the February 1974 general election was called, futher inquiries were put into abeyance.

DTC Working Party

6. In June 1974 the Defence and External Affairs Sub-Committee of Session 1974 eventually took evidence on the information provided[1]. It was then revealed that the Ministry had further responded to the request by carrying out a short study of training arrangements for a number of trades, including the seven under query. The study had been made by the DTC Working Party, an *ad hoc* three-man team comprising one officer from each Service—Commander, RN ; Lieutenant-Colonel, Army ; and Wing Commander, RAF. The Ministry thought that this team, drawn from outside Headquarters, might be more independent in their judgments, and that the staffs of the Directors-General of Training had insufficient time to study training methods and syllabi in the field (Q. 7). Subsequently, the Ministry submitted memoranda summarising the Working Party's inquiries and the DTC's conclusions thereon, and answering further questions arising from the oral evidence[2].

Obstacles to joint training

7. In the course of explaining the activities of the DTC Working Party, the Ministry told the Sub-Committee that there were two main obstacles to joint training (Q. 4). First, they stated that training objectives differ, even for fairly straightforward trades such as cooks and drivers. Second, tailor-made training establishments had been provided, costing millions of pounds to build, and the benefit of these might be lost if joint training involved further building.

8. We accept that these appear at first sight to be major obstacles, but we are not convinced that they are insuperable in the long run. The first point may reflect too ready an acceptance of differences in training objectives, a matter to which we return in paragraphs 10 and 11 : if operational procedures could be wholly or partly standardised it should then be possible to establish common training objectives. We think that their point about tailor-made establishments is more difficult to overcome, but consider that it is an unfortunate consequence of past failure to achieve a joint approach to training. In the case of existing tailor-made establishments their use should be re-examined in relation to their possible use for the joint training needs of more than one Service. As the DTC Working Party recognised in their reports on cooks and helicopter pilots[3], it is most important that the possibility of joint training should be considered before new capital expenditure is incurred. **We therefore recommend that procedures for authorisation of major expenditure on equipment or capital facilities, for training or for other purposes, should include consideration in all cases of the potential requirements of each Service.**

1 Evidence, pages 1-24.
2 Appendices 1–3, pages 54-87.
3 Appendix 3, pages 72-79, Annex A, Appendices 1–2.

9. The Ministry also attach great importance to the single-Service environment as an element in basic training, as experience has shown that recruits wish to be identified with the Service of their choice (Q. 14)[1]. We accept that this is an important point to consider, but we think it quite possible that any disadvantages arising from joint training could be dispelled by skilful presentation and organisation. Moreover, joint training might well foster a competitive spirit which could be harnessed to the training programme, and could improve understanding between the Services, to the ultimate benefit of joint Service operations. Nothing was said by the Ministry to suggest that, in practice, environment has proved to be a disadvantage in any joint training schemes already operating.

Trade training

10. The information provided initially by the Ministry[2] showed significant differences in the Services' approaches to training in apparently similar trades and, as a result, the cost comparisons made were generally qualified. For illustrative purposes we deal with the following five trades or groups of trades:

(i) *Cooks.* The basic training courses for cooks vary in length from 9 weeks (Navy) to 18 weeks (Army) and 19 weeks (RAF)[3]. Following job analysis, the length of the RAF course is being reduced to 14 weeks.[4] The average cost per successful student in 1972–73 varied from £302 (Navy) to £606 (Army) and £1,233 (RAF), although the latter figure was exceptionally high due to a reduction in numbers trained during the RAF manpower economy project. The Ministry explained that the Services' approaches differed according to the degree of supervision required after training and that none of the existing training establishments was large enough to meet all requirements (Q.30–32, 41). Even for advanced cookery training, where the Ministry accepted that the training objectives were similar, and the numbers to be trained were relatively small, the Ministry stated that joint training on a permanent basis would involve additional capital costs (Q. 43)[5]. We note that the DTC Working Party considered that joint training of cooks is not practicable while the Services' training objectives are dissimilar in the standards reached and the degree of supervision given to the cook in his first job[6]. However, we consider that the basic reasons for these dissimilarities may be more apparent than real and should be closely investigated by the Ministry.

(ii) *Clerks and pay clerks.* In the cases of both clerks and pay clerks, the Ministry attributed varying training requirements to differences in operational forms and procedures (Q. 63), a point to which we return in paragraphs 14 and 15 of this Report. Variations exist, for example, in typing speeds required and in the ranges of duties to be covered[7]. There are good reasons for some differences. For instance, Navy clerks are required to act also as pay clerks because accommodation in

---

1 See also Appendix 3, page 72, paragraph 3a.
2 Evidence, pages 1-24.
3 Evidence, page 1, Annex A.
4 Evidence, page 1, Annex A.
5 See also Appendix 2, page 58, paragraph 4.
6 Appendix 3, page 74, Annex A, Appendix 1, paragraph 6a.
7 Evidence, page 2, Annex B.

ships is limited. It is less clear why RAF clerks are trained to a higher basic standard than Army clerks when the former are likely to be employed in locations where advice and supervision are more readily available than they are in Army units. Here again, we believe that the reasons for fundamental differences of this nature should be examined.

(iii) *Vehicle mechanics.* There is a significant difference between the lengths of the basic vehicle mechanic courses in the Army (27 weeks, excluding driving training) and the RAF (13 weeks)[1] which we trust will come under scrutiny in the course of the further studies being undertaken by the Ministry[2]. Following a recommendation by the DTC Working Party, the DTC have decided that the Army should investigate the possibility of co-locating all Service vehicle mechanic training at SEME Bordon[3]. We see this as a step in the right direction and trust that, if co-location proves feasible, it will lead to the early establishment of common training courses. The DTC Working Party concluded that a common course could be devised for Army and Royal Marine requirements, which are very similar, and we consider that this suggestion should be actively pursued.

(iv) *Helicopter pilots.* In this instance, the three basic training courses differ sharply in pattern, a feature which the Ministry attributed mainly to differing operational roles (eg Navy—anti-submarine ; Army—tactical support of ground troops)[4]. Nevertheless, the DTC Working Party considered that there might be scope for partial rationalisation of this training and futher studies are to be made. The Working Party also made the recommendation, which we strongly support, that simulators should be more widely used in order to reduce training costs[5]. We note with interest that the Military Committee of the North Atlantic Assembly has had under consideration the possibility of joint basic training for NATO helicopter pilots, and that the British position has been reserved pending completion of the Defence Review[6]. In principle, we support this concept and we hope that the Ministry will find it possible to take part in this and in other joint training schemes in NATO.

(v) *Medical trades.* In their Seventh Report of Session 1973–74[7], the Expenditure Committee supported the recommendation of the Jarrett Committee that a drive should be made to rationalise as many as possible of the Services' small, separate establishments for specialist medical trade training. In June 1974 the Ministry informed the Sub-Committee that they had decided in principle that laboratory technicians, radiographers and physiotherapists should be trained at one place (Q. 108) but that it had been found impracticable to do the same for dental hygienists and technicians[8]. We welcome the limited progress thus made and hope that more positive plans will quickly emerge even

---

1 Evidence, page 5, Annex C.
2 Appendix 3, page 79, Annex A, Appendix 4.
3 Appendix 3, page 80, Annex A, Appendix 4, paragraph 6.
4 Appendix 3, page 72, paragraph 36.
5 Appendix 3, page 77, Annex A, Appendix 2, paragraph 7.
6 North Atlantic Assembly Document R.176, November 1974.
7 H.C. (1973–74) 168.
8 Appendix 2, pages 60-61, paragraphs 18 and 19.

if, for some reason, action cannot be taken at an early date. In the case of "medical orderlies", we note that the DTC Working Party accepted the Ministry's view that the operational needs of the Services are so different that joint training should not be pursued, and that the DTC concluded that joint training was neither desirable nor practicable[1]. We remain somewhat sceptical about this conclusion since there must be a fair degree of commonality in the courses as a whole even if there are differences in emphasis. We also doubt whether the arguments adduced by the Ministry would apply with equal force to Service training of female nurses.

11. We consider that the DTC Working Party's inquiries have yielded a number of constructive suggestions and recommendations, some of which have already been mentioned. Although progress so far has been fairly slow, these results have shown, in contrast to the Ministry's earlier pessimistic view, that improvements can still be found which could lead to useful recurrent savings. Given a more fundamental approach to the question why training objectives differ, we believe that a renewed drive could produce further potential savings. We suggest that the trades already examined should be looked at in a new light, and no doubt there are very many other trades common to more than one Service where the same techniques can be applied. An example of a trade which might be probed is that of musician ; at a time when Service manpower is declining, and the number of military bands is likely to follow suit, it seems appropriate to question whether three separate Service schools of music should still be maintained[2]. **We therefore recommend that the DTC Working Party should be reconstituted and strengthened, that their terms of reference and scope of studies should be extended to include full critical study of the operational and environmental reasons for differences in training objectives and that their suggestions and recommendations should be vigorously pursued.**

Existing unified or joint training schemes

12. The Ministry gave a number of examples of unified or joint training schemes which are in operation. They stated that in most cases these schemes had been implemented primarily in the interest of efficiency to provide the best possible training resources for personnel to fulfil the specific needs of each of the three Services[3]. The Ministry were surprisingly unable to quantify any cost savings which might have accrued. Much greater attention should be paid to identifying cost savings in joint service training schemes.

13. From the examples given, we infer that unified or joint training has operated mainly in fairly specialised fields, where the numbers under training are generally small. We also note that in two instances, the Defence NBC School and Defence Explosive Ordnance Disposal, sixteen and nine years, respectively, elapsed from the start of joint Service training until all three Services were brought fully into the arrangements. This may reflect an unduly cautious approach, and we hope that much quicker progress will be made with future schemes.

---

1 Appendix 3, page 78, Annex A, Appendix 3.
2 H.C. Deb. Vol. 875, Cols. 510–11 (Written).
3 Evidence, page 11, Annex B; Appendix 2, page 69, Annex A.

Pay and records

14. The Ministry informed the Sub-Committee that computerisation has led to considerable savings in the Services (Q. 66). Each of the Services maintains its own computer system for pay and for management record-keeping but the three systems were introduced at varying dates and employ different machines[1]. The machines currently in use are due for replacement in 1976 (RAF), 1978–79 (Navy) and 1979–80 (Army) and there are no plans to replace them with one installation. The Ministry stated that their aim is computer compatibility, with attendant benefits including the availability of alternative computing resources in an emergency, rather than provision of one installation for three separate pay and records systems[2]. We consider that the aim should be to provide a unified Services' pay and records system on one computer installation if possible.

15. We note that the DTC Working Party concluded that the real difficulty in rationalising pay clerk training lies in the fact that terminology, documentation and administrative procedures differ widely between the Services and that until the Services are in a position to introduce common procedures, unification of the training of pay clerks is not feasible[3]. In view of this conclusion we regret that no timetable has been fixed yet for standardisation of Service pay and records forms and procedures. The objections advanced against the production of a single set of pay regulations[4] seem to us to rest too heavily on preservation of single-Service terminology and practices, and we cannot believe that it is impossible to solve the problems involved. A Committee has been appointed to review the pay and records systems and to consider the extent to which they might be developed on similar lines, compatible with the individual requirements of the three Services for pay and record information[5]. We believe that this approach avoids the main issue. **We therefore recommend that the pay and records committee should be instructed to take as their primary objective the preparation of a plan for the early introduction in the Services of common forms, procedures and regulations for pay and personnel documentation. We further recommend that a survey of computer installations should be undertaken urgently and that nothing should be done in the short-term to prejudice the objective of a common computer system. We also recommend that the pay and records committee should seek advice and assistance from the Civil Service Department, or other independent authority.** An independent observer might well bring fresh ideas to bear on the subject and act as a catalyst in the solution of what has seemed to be an intractable problem.

Job analysis

16. We were informed of impressive savings in training times achieved by the use of job analysis techniques[6], although we note that the three Services do not use similar methods. For example, CODAP, a new and successful system used by the Navy, has been demonstrated to the Army, but not apparently to the RAF[7]. In a related field, we note that the DTC Working Party found that the Army have been successfully using a programmed instruction method of

---

1 Appendix 2, page 68, paragraph 38.
2 Appendix 2, page 68, paragraph 41.
3 Appendix 3, page 80. Annex A, Appendix 5.
4 Appendix 2, page 69, paragraph 44.
5 Appendix 2, page 69, paragraph 42.
6 Appendix 2, pages 61–66, paragraphs 24–30.
7 Appendix 2, page 62, paragraph 29.

training clerks ; the Working Party recommended, and the DTC agreed, that this method should be considered by the other Services[1].

Conclusions

17. Although our inquiries have focussed mainly on trade training, the subject should not be considered in isolation. We envisage that a fresh approach to common problems in the Services could reach into the potentially more rewarding area of operational and administrative procedures, and could lead eventually to substantial recurrent savings. We believe that a new and powerful initiative must come from the Ministry's Central Staffs to question, and challenge, established practices throughout the Services. As we have already made clear, we cannot accept that joint training is necessarily ruled out when existing training objectives differ ; our view is that the operational reasons for differing training objectives should be thoroughly investigated to see in what respects they could be brought together. We recognise that such an approach may lead to some loss of single-Service autonomy, but this would be well justified if overheads could thereby be cut to the ultimate benefit of the fighting arms.

18. The Ministry have stated that intakes at training establishments may be affected by the results of the Defence Review, and that the question of joint training of common administrative grades will be examined in the light of the outcome of the Review[2]. Some changes of the kinds which we have in mind may well be inevitable in the wake of the Defence Review, particularly in those areas most affected by the proposed reductions in manpower. But as the results of the Review seem likely in the main to reflect major policy changes, we believe that positive action is needed to supplement the Review. While a reconstituted DTC Working Party should provide much useful material, we propose that their activities should form an important part of a wider study of methods and practices which might cover, for example, standards of manning and of equipment, stores control methods and procedures, and management techniques.

19. **We therefore recommend that, co-extensively with the re-constitution of the DTC Working Party referred to in paragraph 11, the Ministry of Defence should carry out a wide-ranging examination of operational, administrative and training activities to seek out long-term recurrent economies which might arise from the adoption by the Services of a common approach to procedures, documentation, training courses and possibly, in some areas, Headquarters organisation.** We consider that responsibility for co-ordinating this task should be placed upon a very senior official, or group of officials, at the centre of the Ministry, under the direction of a Minister, who should be empowered to call on outside advice in specialist fields and to examine the facts at first hand across Service boundaries.

RAF MANPOWER ECONOMY PROJECT

20. In the last Defence White Paper before the current Defence Review, attention was drawn to a major review of Royal Air Force manpower and support requirements which was expected to result in a reduction of some 6,000

1 Appendix 3, page 82, Annex A, Appendix 6, paragraph 5.
2 Appendix 3, page 72, paragraph 4.

posts without detriment to the front line[1]. Since manpower costs represent 47 per cent. of defence spending overall, savings in manpower, are extremely important in keeping defence expenditure within reasonable limits. We therefore decided to examine the project to establish how it had come about, how effective it had been, and what lessons might be drawn for wider application.

Origins and purposes of the project

21. The RAF began their manpower economy project in 1971. Its inception sprang from the conviction that an increasing part of the RAF's budget was being devoted to support or tail functions to the detriment of the front line or teeth of the Service. It was clear that if the pressure of manpower costs could be reduced, the weapon procurement programme would be more easily sustained (Q. 120). The initiative came from within the RAF and apparently owed much to the then C. in C. RAF Strike Command who conducted a short experiment in Strike Command (Q. 111). With support from the Air Force Board, the manpower review was then applied throughout the Service. The exercise was conducted through the normal chains of command with only a small team specifically directing the project on a permanent basis (Q. 112–13). Targets for savings were set, and each Station Commander was encouraged to suggest how economies could be attained within his command (Q. 114). Suggestions were sought from all levels within the Service. The resulting savings achieved by the RAF were substantial and widespread.

Results of the project

22. In a memorandum submitted in August 1974[2], the Ministry of Defence confirmed that since 1971, 5,872 Service and 1,471 civilian posts had been given up, providing recurrent savings, the annual value of which amounted to about £18·5 millions. These savings, which represent overall cuts of approximately 5·4 per cent. in Service manpower and 3·1 per cent. in civilian manpower in the RAF, were absorbed mainly by normal wastage, voluntary retirements and adjustments in recruiting and re-engagement levels. A limited redundancy programme was also necessary involving about 500 officers and 900 men (Q. 133). The RAF emphasised that these manpower reductions did not impair operational efficiency in any way (Q. 140).

23. The project was managed in two separate phases[3]. Phase I consisted of a campaign throughout the RAF to indentify posts which could be disestablished without unacceptable risks, changes of policy or loss of efficiency ; and reductions were made in most establishments in the Service. During Phase II the RAF sought to achieve economies in manpower mainly through reviewing policies, tasks, operations and procedures in order to reduce manpower and support costs to the minimum. The initial Phase was essentially a squeeze on manpower across the board. In Phase II, however, there were many individual savings[4]. Examples of the specific economies made include : redeployment of training tasks to allow the closure of RAF Manby and RAF Spitalgate ; tape recording of aircraft communications for investigation of aircraft incidents ; revision of ground radio servicing procedures to use manpower more effectively ;

---

[1] Published in February 1973, Cmnd. 5231, page 26, paragraph 20, and page 33, paragraph 26.
[2] Evidence, pages 39–41.
[3] Evidence, page 40, paragraph 4.
[4] Evidence, pages 39–41.

reduction of training staff for apprentice entry schemes following the raising of the school leaving age ; reduction in the number of aircrews required for Nimrod squadrons ; the merging of Maintenance Command and No. 90 Group into Support Command ; the streamlining of Training Command ; and amalgamation of the Directorates-General of Engineering and Supply to form a Controllerate of Engineering and Supply. Most of these savings have been achieved within the framework of existing facilities with relatively little new capital expenditure.

Role of the Central Staffs of the Ministry of Defence

24. We were particularly concerned, in our consideration of the RAF economies, with the role played by the Central Staffs of the Ministry of Defence. In a previous Report in 1974[1] the Expenditure Committee commented on the organisation of the Ministry which allows each Service considerable autonomy. Nevertheless, we were disappointed to learn that although the inception of the RAF manpower project was known at a high level throughout the Ministry of Defence, it was initiated and prosecuted solely by the Air Force Department, and the Central Staffs were not significantly involved[2]. The potential savings arising from the review were such that the centre should have paid the closest attention to the progress being made by the RAF. We do not accept the Ministry's claim that such attention might have inhibited the efforts being made by the RAF (Q. 161). Moreover, it might have provided the Central Staffs with valuable lessons which could have been applied in similar systematic reviews of Headquarters', Navy and Army manpower.

25. In the light of the impressive results yielded by the RAF review, of which the Ministry were well aware, it is surprising that the centre did not feel that the Royal Navy and the Army could have been stimulated to mount similar projects, especially by means of the scrutiny of tasks as carried out by the RAF in Phase II. We consider that the role of the Central Staffs should not be limited solely to the allocation of resources as suggested in evidence (Q. 177) but also, as a minimum requirement, should be directed to securing optimum standards of management within the Services. The present arrangements go little beyond the federal structure created by the amalgamation of the Service Departments in the Ministry of Defence in 1964. We recommend below that henceforth the centre should be more closely involved in the management of the individual Services.

Manpower economies in the other Services

26. Since the RAF took the initiative in instituting their review of manpower, it is for consideration whether each of the other Services could have undertaken a similar exercise. It was well known to the Royal Navy and the Army that the RAF project was in progress (Q. 177), but for a number of reasons neither Service followed the RAF's example. The Navy and the Army were experiencing great difficulty in meeting recruiting targets, which resulted in stringent standards of manning (Q. 162), and they were not quite so concerned with the ratio of teeth to tail as the RAF with its small numbers in the front line. Both Services, in the period of the RAF review, were re-organising their Commands and various other activities (Q. 178, 184). Nonetheless, the percentage reductions in manpower achieved by the Royal Navy and the Army during the period from

---

[1] Seventh Report from the Expenditure Committee, Session 1973–74, H.C. (1973–74) 168.
[2] Evidence, pages 41–43.

1971–72 to 1974–75 compare unfavourably with the achievements of the RAF. While all Services show significant decreases, the RAF achieved similar reductions to those achieved by the other Services in addition to the savings attributed to the manpower economy project. Total RAF savings between 1971–72 and 1974–75 amounted to approximately $11 \cdot 2^1$ per cent. of all manpower, compared with $6 \cdot 3$ per cent. for the Navy and $5 \cdot 6$ per cent. for the Army over the same period[2].

27. The Royal Navy have been obliged to keep manpower levels under review by recurrent shortfalls in recruiting targets for some years. Manpower shortages, especially in technical grades, led to the introduction in 1972 of a system of manpower allocation[3]. The system relates annually the total manpower requirement to the forecast availability, and tasks of lowest priority are then given up. By April 1975 about 500 Naval posts ashore will have been disestablished. More generally the Command structures of the Navy were rationalised under one Home and one Sea Command. Considerable manpower savings have resulted from these and other measures (Q. 178). Although worthwhile savings were thus achieved, we believe that a concerted drive on the lines of the RAF project might have given even better results.

28. The Ministry of Defence have stated that Army manpower is controlled by the allocation of officers and soldiers to approved tasks closely screened by the Army's machinery for manpower accounting and establishment inspection and review (Q. 184)[4]. Moreover, recruitment shortfalls have effectively limited the manpower available. No special manpower review has been considered necessary in recent years since several major re-organisations have been undertaken including the completion of the new UK Land Forces Command Structure ; the re-organisation of the Army's Manning and Record Offices saving 560 civilian posts since 1967 ; the introduction of the RAOC computer-based Central Inventory for supplies and provisioning ; and the re-organisation of junior training between 1969 and 1973 saving 250 Service and 350 civilian posts. In evidence it was admitted that a comprehensive study of the kind undertaken by the RAF had not been attempted by the Army (Q. 184). As in the case of the Navy, we must conclude that a full scale manpower review would probably yield further substantial savings.

Defence Review

29. It would not be appropriate to examine the manpower policies of the Services without considering the effect on those policies of the cuts in Service manpower proposed as part of the Defence Review. In his statement to the House on 3rd December 1974, the Secretary of State for Defence said that over the next ten years the RAF would sustain a cut of 18,000 Servicemen, while the Army and Navy would lose 12,000 and 5,000, respectively ; there was also to be a reduction of 30,000 civilian posts[5]. The reduction of 18,000 was tentatively attributable to a cutting of tasks allotted to the RAF, and RAF witnesses did not feel at any disadvantage in facing the Defence Review following their man-

---

1 Of this total, approximately $4 \cdot 6$ per cent. relates to the manpower economy project and $6 \cdot 6$ per cent. to other savings.
2 These figures are derived from published Estimates.
3 Evidence, page 42, paragraph 3.
4 Evidence, pages 41–42, paragraph 1.
5 H.C. Deb. Vol. 882, Cols. 1351–57, 1366.

power economies (Q. 143–45). We do not argue that, if their commitments are cut, the RAF should not make the manpower cuts allocated in the Review. But it seems likely that, following their previous efforts, the RAF may find it much more difficult than the other Services to achieve the target manpower reductions set in the Defence Review.

Conclusions

30. The RAF manpower economy project appears to have been an extremely well-conducted review of manpower and its deployment in the RAF. The resulting recurrent savings are substantial and have been achieved without loss of efficiency (Q. 140). We recognise the perception and initiative shown by all concerned with the project and that the record of the RAF contrasts favourably with those of the other two Services. While the Navy and Army have saved substantial numbers of posts and re-organised their Command structures during the same period, we cannot avoid the conclusion that had they reviewed their policies and tasks systematically as was done in Phase II of the RAF project, considerably greater savings in manpower might have been achieved. We trust that the lessons of the RAF project will be comprehensively applied during the squeeze on manpower which will inevitably accompany the implementation of the Defence Review.

31. We consider that, even more than the Navy and Army, the Central Staffs of the Ministry of Defence should implement elsewhere the lessons of the RAF manpower project. No part of the defence budget can be seen in isolation from the remainder. Savings made on manpower in one Service should, in an integrated defence budget, be available to meet the most pressing military need. In this context it is a basic interest of the Ministry of Defence that all three Services should be manned and organised as efficiently as possible. In evidence it was stated that the role of the centre is to allocate resources, but that management is left to the Service Boards (Q. 177). We cannot accept that the centre should ignore the need for uniform standards of management and organisation in the Services. **We therefore recommend that the Central Staffs of the Ministry of Defence should establish common manning standards to be applied, where appropriate, in making the reductions in manpower set by the Defence Review.**

GENERAL CONCLUSIONS

32. In connection with both Service training and the RAF manpower economy project we regret the passive role played by the Ministry's Central Staffs. Although amalgamation of the former Service Ministries in the Ministry of Defence took place more than ten years ago, many features of the previous structure remain. In essence, the Central Staffs now co-ordinate from within instead of from a separate Ministry. We believe that the Central Staffs must be given a much more positive role in fostering a common approach to many problems which are handled at present almost exclusively on a single-Service basis, and that they should have power to determine a joint course of action where this seems justified.

33. An example of joint Service activity which was initially discounted by the Ministry is the amalgamation of the posts of Command Secretary, BAOR

and Financial Adviser, RAF Germany. In February 1972 the Expenditure Committee recommended that consideration should be given to merging these posts with a view to avoiding duplication and to economising on administrative services[1]. The Committee had been told that the corresponding posts in Cyprus had been merged, but that the two Headquarters in Germany were not fully integrated and it would be difficult to adopt a system whereby one Command Secretary handled both Services. In July 1972 the Ministry replied that amalgamation was feasible but problems to be overcome included minor differences in Service administration and complications arising from NATO responsibilities ; they thought that any joint organisation would need to provide at all levels for the specialised requirements and separate identities of the two Services, and that amalgamation would not result in any significant staff savings[2]. Subsequently, the Committee were informed that the two posts in Germany were combined on 1st January 1974 and that a single organisation now served the two single-Service Headquarters[3]. This is an example of the kind of reform which we are keen to see introduced, and which we hope will lead to considerable recurrent savings as greater experience is gained of joint administration of support and welfare services.

34. The Expenditure Committee commented in their Seventh Report of Session 1973–74[4] that unification at Heaquarters level of the three Services would not be inconsistent with the present separation at most other levels. This is not an argument for complete integration of the Services themselves, and we fully accept the need to maintain three separate fighting Services. But at a time when the Services as a whole are contracting, and economic pressures are mounting, we are persuaded that major changes are inevitable and must be accepted if fighting efficiency is to remain as a first charge on the defence budget. Our inquiries have convinced us that long-term benefits would flow from a policy of greater central direction and control of the Services. The centre already arbitrates in the allocation of resources to the Services, but in so doing, it must also be satisfied that those resources are employed to the best advantage.

35. **We therefore recommend that the role and functions of the Ministry's Central Staffs should now be strengthened as part of the process of developing an efficient organisation for the control, management and administration of the Services. The objective would be to achieve better control of the use of resources, to ensure active co-operation in matters of manpower planning, training and management, and to effect harmonisation of administrative procedures and organisations.**

---

1 Second Report from the Expenditure Committee, Session 1971–72, H.C. (1971–72) 141, paragraph 47.
2 Fifth Special Report from the Expenditure Committee, Session 1971–72, H.C. (1971–72) 451, paragraph 12.
3 Ministry letter dated 11th January, 1974 (not reported).
4 Seventh Report from the Expenditure Committee, Session 1973–74, H.C. (1973–74) 168, paragraph 17.

LIST OF WITNESSES

SESSION 1974

SESSION 1974–75

MEMORANDA INCLUDED IN THE MINUTES OF EVIDENCE

APPENDICES TO THE MINUTES OF EVIDENCE

MINUTES OF EVIDENCE TAKEN BEFORE THE EXPENDITURE COMMITTEE (DEFENCE AND EXTERNAL AFFAIRS SUB-COMMITTEE)

SESSION 1974

TUESDAY, 18TH JUNE, 1974

Members present:

Mr. James Boyden	Mr. Geoffrey Finsberg
Mr. Bernard Conlan	Dr. Maurice Miller
Major-General d'Avigdor-Goldsmid	Mr. John Roper

In the absence of the Chairman Mr. James Boyden was called to the Chair.

TRAINING (D.1)
Memorandum by the Ministry of Defence (SCOE 31/9/2/1)

1. The Sub-Committee has asked for papers on the comparative costs to each Service for the training of:

(a) Cooks

(b) Clerical Staff

(c) Vehicle Mechanics

(d) Pay Clerks

(e) Helicopter Pilots

(f) Drivers

(g) Medical Orderlies.

2. It was explained in Memorandum SCOE 31/9/2 that medical orderlies are no longer employed in the Services and there are insufficient similarities in the replacing trades to enable a useful comparison of their training costs to be made.

3. Details of the trades listed in paragraph 1 above, with the exception of medical orderlies, are set out at Annexes A to F of this Memorandum. The costings are based on the financial year 1972-73 and in each instance a brief description is given of the trade in question, together with course length, the number of successful students, the assessed cost of the particular course (or part of course) and the per capita training cost.

4. In making comparisons of per capita costs, the following considerations need to be borne in mind:

(a) the trades which the Sub-Committee has selected are broadly analogous but the duties involved vary from Service to Service—training is arranged to fit the man for the particular Service task he will be undertaking;

(b) the duties of one Service trade can be much wider than those of the most comparable trade in another service; in some cases, it has been necessary to adopt the device of comparing one part of one Service's course with the whole of another's:

(c) the length of training and the standard to be achieved, even in analogous trades, is determined by the extent to which further training either on the job or formal, is planned in the tradesman's career;

(d) Every endeavour has been made to ensure that the costings in the Annexes attached have been done on a comparable basis. Inevitably, however, *complete uniformity is not possible* when one sets out to cost establishments that are part of different organisations. Judgments have to be made about the allocation of costs and the attribution of overheads. Variations arise primarily because of the special circumstances in which training is carried out at a particular establishment. Some variation is due to the *different accounting conventions* applied in the three Services although so far as is possible the same conditions have been applied over the whole field.

5. These considerations underline the difficulty in obtaining direct comparisons of per capita training costs. A further qualification has to be made in respect of the figures quoted for RAF training. The costings relate to the last complete financial year, 1972–73. Because of the impact of a major review of RAF manpower and support requirements, the year is unrepresentative of normal RAF training activity. Recruitment had been cut back severely but the redeployment of training resources, to match revised tasks, had not been implemented. Thus, temporarily, an abnormally low level of training activity attracted unduly high overhead costs. When the Service is more in balance there should be a sharp reduction in per capita training costs.

ANNEX A

TRAINING OF COOKS

Royal Navy

1. RN/WRNS cooks are trained on a basic course of 9 weeks at HMS PEMBROKE, Chatham. The training is mainly devoted to practical cookery but also includes some general service training. It is designed to produce a rating capable of carrying out the duties of a cook in HM Ships and Establishments after completion of further on the job training under supervision in a shore establishment. The annual cost of training cooks at HMS PEMBROKE is £117,000. HMS PEMBROKE also runs several other administrative courses, is a Fleet Accommodation Centre, and provides support facilities for the Fleet Maintenance Group, Craft Maintenance Support, Reserve Ships, and the Staff of the Flag Officer Medway.

Royal Marines

2. RM Cooks are trained on the RN basic course at HMS PEMBROKE alongside RN/WRNS ratings, but spend their last week's training at CTCRM Lympstone in field cookery. The training is designed to produce cooks for RM Units and establishments who can, when necessary, cook under operational conditions using established or improvised field cooking equipment.

3. The total annual cost of training RM cooks is £15,400, which includes the annual costs of the one week field training at Lympstone of £3,084.

Army

4. Army cooks are drawn from the Army Catering Corps (ACC) and the WRAC. Their training takes place at ST OMER BARRACKS, Aldershot which runs courses designed to train ACC and All Arms students in Service Catering. The basic cookery course is 18 weeks mainly in practical cookery, but it also includes aspects of military training and leads to a BIII standard.

5. The trained cook is required to have a practical and theoretical knowledge of meal preparation, pastry, butchery, larder work, and field cookery. The cost of basic cookery training amounts to £280,950, including WRAC cooks.

Royal Air Force

6. The trade training of RAF Cooks, which at present lasts 19 weeks, is carried out at RAF HEREFORD. The course teaches kitchen practice, cooking methods, preparation, butchery, field cookery, hygiene, by-products, in-flight feeding, work organisation, catering equipment, portion out and stock control, catering administration and bulk cooking. There is also a small element of general service training.

7. *RAF Hereford,* like other RAF training establishments, was affected by the manpower review to which reference has been made in para 5 of the Memorandum. Thus the RAF's per capita training cost for cooks was, in 1972–73, much greater than would be normal. Apart from the reversion to a more usual level of training in 1974–75, the transfer of the WRAF Recruit Training Depot from RAF SPITALGATE to RAF HEREFORD, so reducing the share of fixed support costs allocated to cook's training, should further reduce the per capita cost. In addition the Royal Air Force has recently carried out a job analysis of the trade of cook, and as a result a new basic course reduced from 19 to 14 weeks is to be introduced; specialist aspects such as butchery and in-flight feeding will no longer be taught.

8. The present annual cost of training RAF basic cooks is £76,215.

9. SUMMARY

Service and Trade	RN/WRNS Cook	RM Cook	ARMY Cook	WRAC Cook	RAF/WRAF Cook
Length of course ...	9 weeks (1)	9 weeks (2)	18 weeks	16 weeks (3)	19 weeks
Number trained per annum	387	50	407	80	62
Cost per successful student 1972–73 ...	£302	£308	£606	£424	£1,233
Total cost per annum 1972–73	£117,000	£15,400	£246,780	£34,170	£76,215

NOTES:

1. RN/WRNS cooks are given further on the job training before being considered fully trained.

2. RM cooks undertake one week's field cookery course at Lympstone.

3. WRAC cooks do not complete the 2 weeks field training courses undergone by men.

ANNEX B

TRAINING OF CLERICAL STAFF

Royal Navy

1. Clerical work in the Royal Navy is carried out by the RN Writers who are trained in both secretarial/administrative duties and pay/cash duties; there are no separate trades of clerk and pay clerk. The 11 week writer course consists of 8 weeks training in pay/cash duties and 3 weeks in secretarial/administrative duties. The trained writer is capable of performing general clerical duties, with correspondence, personnel records and typing as well as pay and cash accounting in a ship or shore establishment.

2. The training is carried out at the Royal Naval Supply School, HMS PEMBROKE, Chatham which also undertakes other training and administrative functions. The annual cost of the 3 weeks secretarial/administration training is estimated at £12,100.

Royal Marines

3. The Royal Marines train their Grade 3 clerks in Basic Clerical Duties and Typing on a 2 week course which enables them to type at 15 wpm, operate and maintain office machinery and provide a basic knowledge of the RM organisation and their associated office procedures. After 6 months on the job training they will, if successful, be eligible to be graded as a Clerk (Pay and Records) (CPR) Grade 3 or Clerk (Quartermaster) Grade 3.

4. The training is carried out at the Commando Training Centre LYMPSTONE where more than 30 other training courses are held including those for Young Officers, NCOs and Recruits. The annual cost of the RM Basic Clerical Duties and Typing course is approximately £5,700.

Army

5. The Army use a programme learning system of teaching to train Clerks (General Duties) and this enables the soldier to complete the course in 2 to 5 weeks. The average course length is 2½ weeks.

6. The student is required to type at 15 wpm and familiarise himself with office machinery and basic office procedures. The training, to Army BIII standard, is aimed at Company HQ level where practical training continues until after twelve months on the job training he may attain BII standard. He may return to the training school at a later stage for more advanced training to BI standard.

7. This training is carried out at the RAOC Training Centre, BLACKDOWN CAMP, Deepcut, which also offers a wide range of other courses for RAOC and All Arms personnel. The annual cost of training Clerks (GD) to BIII standard is approximately £202,000.

Royal Air Force

8. The RAF employ Clerks Secretarial whose training syllabus includes a large element of practical training (40 hours are spent in an office simulator), and typing to a speed of 25 wpm. The trainee is required to take final examinations in theory and practical clerical work which will fit the successful student for a world-wide posting without further training. On reporting to his first unit the Clerk Secretarial can expect to work under supervision for a short time and provided he passes an appropriate examination he will be promoted to SAC. Further promotion is not governed by more trade training.

9. The RAF Clerk Secretarial is trained at No 3 School of Technical Training RAF HEREFORD where more than 30 other training courses are held for grades including cooks, mess stewards, catering officers, and a variety of other clerical grades. The annual cost of training Clerks Secretarial is £47,000.

10. Reference has been made in the Memorandum and in Annex A to the under-utilisation of RAF HEREFORD'S training resources in 1972–73 and of the expectation of more cost-effective operation in the future. In addition to the consequences of a more normal training activity and of the move of the WRAF Depot, a proposal to amalgamate the duties of the Clerk Secretarial and the Clerk Accounting is under consideration and, if decided upon, may permit a single training course to replace 2 existing courses with further reduction in per capita costs.

11. The RAF Clerk Secretarial course is longer and much more detailed in content than those of the other Services and equips the Clerk Secretarial for the work he will be required to do without undertaking additional training courses. The RAF Clerk Secretarial is for instance trained to the same standard as the Army BI clerk for which a period of on the job training and a further training course is necessary qualification. For this reason, coupled with under-utilisation of resources, the per capita cost of training an RAF Clerk Secretarial in 1972–73 was much higher than the cost of training men for analogous tasks in the other Services.

12.   CLERKS SECRETARIAL

Service & Trade	RN Writers (Secretarial/ Adm. Duties)	RM Clerk (QM) or (Pay & Records)	Army (Clerks GD)	RAF (Clerk Secretarial)
Length of course	3 weeks (1)	2 weeks	2/5 weeks (average 2½ weeks)	9 weeks
Number trained (annual) ...	144	65	1,482	102
Cost per successful student 1972–73	£84	£88	£136	£460
Total cost (annual) 1972–73	£12,100	£5,700	£202,000	£47,000

NOTE:

1. This is part of the 11 week training course for RN writers.

ANNEX C

TRAINING OF VEHICLE MECHANICS

Royal Navy

1. The RN does not have a trade of vehicle mechanic. Repairs to Navy vehicles are carried out by industrial civil servants.

Royal Marines

2. The RM employs vehicle mechanics. The syllabus for their training is broadly similar to that of the Army but differs from the RAF in so far as RM mechanics are taught to drive whilst RAF Trainees are not.

3. An RM mechanic is required to inspect, maintain, and carry out major repairs in the field to all Group B vehicles held by a Commando. These are land vehicles of all types which are not primarily designed for offensive purposes but which may in some cases, be armoured for defensive purposes. This may include land vehicles built to General Service or commercial specifications. An RM mechanic is also trained to maintain and repair oversnow vehicles, and outboard motors held by the Royal Marines. The training is carried out at RM POOLE Dorset, which also undertakes RM landing craft and special boat, ship's detachment, and technical training.

4. The annual cost of the Vehicle Mechanic Course is £49,478.

Army

5. The Army's Vehicle Mechanics are trained at the School of Electrical and Mechanical Engineering (SEME) at BORDON, Hants. Here also are trained all ranks of the Royal Electrical and Mechanical Engineers (REME) in the theory, practice and equipment technology required in the recovery, inspection, modification, and repair of the Army's electro-mechanical equipment.

6. At BORDON, Army vehicle mechanics are trained on a 31 week course to a point where they are capable of going on to advanced equipment and military training.

7. The annual cost of vehicle mechanic training is £657,050.

Royal Air Force

8. The Royal Air Force vehicle mechanic training syllabus differs from those of the RM and Army in that the RAF does not train its mechanics to drive nor does it expect them to be able to do so. The mobility of the RM and Army demands that their personnel should drive: in the RAF there is no such need.

9. RAF training is carried out at No 4 School of Technical Training (4SofTT) which is a Training Command unit "lodging" at RAF ST ATHAN, a station in Support Command. 4SofTT conducts 75 types of courses each year in the fields of aircraft engineering, mechanical transport, safety and surface, *physical training*, and the quality assurance service. The annual cost of training vehicle mechanics in the RAF is £17,870.

Costs

10. The comparison of training costs is given below, but it should be remembered that this comparison is not strictly like with like because each Service requires a different end product:

Service	RM Vehicle Mechanic	Army Vehicle Mechanic	RAF MT Mechanic
Length of Course	33 weeks (1)	31 weeks (2)	13 weeks (3)
Number trained per annum	34	463	29
Cost per man trained 1972–73 ...	£1,455 (4)	£1,417 (5)	£615 (6)
Total cost per annum 1972–73 ...	£49,478	£657,050	£17,870

NOTES:

   1. Includes 6 weeks driving training.

   2. Includes 4 weeks driving training.

   3. Does not include driving training.

   4. Cost of 6 weeks driving training is £596.

   5. Cost of 4 weeks driving training is £370. All driver training is given on Heavy Goods Vehicles, type B. Light vehicles are not used for training.

   6. Some 50 per cent of RAF mechanics return to school for Fitter training after about 2 years experience as MT mechanics.

ANNEX D

TRAINING OF PAY CLERKS

Royal Navy

   1. The RN does not have a separate trade of pay clerk. All RN writers may be called upon to perform pay/cash duties, and their 11 week writers' training course includes an eight week training period on pay/cash duties.

   2. Training is carried out at the Royal Navy Supply School, HMS PEMBROKE, Chatham which runs other courses and undertakes several administrative functions. The annual cost of this 8 week pay/cash training is estimated at £31,400.

Royal Marines

   3. The Royal Marines employ Pay and Records Clerks and their training qualifies them to carry out pay duties, on the RN system, and to maintain RM records, which differ from other Service records, in Company Offices and in Unit Imprest and Record Offices.

   4. This work is carried out at the basic level by Clerks after a 2 weeks' course and 6 months on the job training as detailed in Annex B, paragraph 3. The costs of this course are detailed in the Table in Annex B.

Army

   5. The Royal Army Pay Corps as well as staffing large static pay offices provides clerks for pay work in Army units world-wide.

   6. Their training is carried out at the Royal Army Pay Corps Training Centre, WORTHY DOWN, which also conducts a variety of other courses in financial matters including ADP, cost accountancy, non-public funds and upgrading courses. The annual cost of training pay clerks to Army BIII grading, a standard comparable with their counterparts in the other Services, is £33,000.

Royal Air Force

   7. The RAF employs a grade of Clerk Accounting whose training provides instruction on airmen's pay, allowances and cash accounting. On successful completion of training, Clerks Accounting are posted for duty as Leading Aircraftsmen, when their standard of proficiency it broadly analogous to their counterparts in the other Services.

   8. Training is carried out at No 3 School of Technical Training RAF HEREFORD which also runs some 30 other types of training courses for such grades as cooks, mess stewards, and catering officers as well as for other clerical grades. The annual cost of training Clerks Accounting is assessed at £19,572.

   9. Reference has been made in the Memorandum and in Annexes A and B to the root causes of under-utilisation of RAF training resources in 1972–73, to the expectation of more cost-effective operation and to the consequences of a possible amalgamation of the trades of Clerk Accounting and Clerk Secretariat.

Summary

   10. The comparative costs for the training of Pay Clerks in the three Services are as follows:

Service and Trade	RN Writer (Pay/Cash Duties)	Army Pay Clerk RAPC	RAF Clerk Accounting
Length of Course	8 weeks (1)	7 weeks	8 weeks
Number trained per annum	144	106	52
Cost per man trained 1972–73... ...	£218	£313	£380
Total cost (per annum) 1972–73 ...	£31,400	£33,000	£19,572

NOTE:

1. This is part of the 11 week training course for RN Writers.

ANNEX E

TRAINING OF HELICOPTER PILOTS

General

1. Each Service trains its Pilots to operate particular types of aircraft in its own appropriate roles. There is however a broadly similar pattern followed by all three Services, viz:

Initial Training on Fixed Wing (FW) Aircraft

Basic Helicopter Rotary Wing (RW) Training

Advanced Helicopter Training

Within that pattern there are two important variations in that for selection to future aircraft type and career purposes the RAF train all pilots to "wings" standard on FW Aircraft and there is a requirement for the Naval pilot to have an early introduction to instrument flight.

2. Pilot applicants are tested for flying aptitude and medical fitness before starting Initial Flying Training. If successful, trainees start the FW phase which provides the basic flying and airmanship skills needed for later training. In the second of these phases —Basic RW Training—the student pilot is converted to and taught to handle and navigate a simple type of helicopter, which provides him with sufficient expertise to qualify for the advanced phase of his training. It is the basic RW Course for each Service which has been used for the purpose of this paper as providing training comparability.

Royal Navy

3. Basic RW training is carried out at RNAS CULDROSE where the course lasts 10 weeks (50 days) and includes 49 hours flying instruction on Hiller Rotary Wing aircraft. RNAS CULDROSE also carries out other training as well as operational tasks. In 1972–73, 62 students successfully completed the Basic RW Course at a total cost of £557,000 or £9,000 per student. Before starting this course, students will have completed 75 hours on Fixed Wing aircraft at RAF CHURCH FENTON.

Army

4. Basic RW training is carried out at the Army Aviation Centre (AAC) MIDDLE WALLOP. The course lasts 14 weeks (70 days) and includes 80 hours flying instruction on Bell 64 aircraft. In 1972–73, 45 students successfully completed the course at a total cost of some £503,000 or £11,200 per student. Before starting the course, students complete a Basic FW course including 40 hours flying, also carried out at Middle Wallop.

Royal Air Force

5. Following their Basic FW training to "Wings" standard (total flying hours 175), selected pilots undergo Basic RW training at RAF TERN HILL. The course lasts 9 weeks (45 days) and includes 46 hours flying on Sioux aircraft. In 1972–73, 42 students successfully completed the course at a total cost of £438,000 or £10,400 per student. RAF TERN HILL carries out various other flying training (including the training of RW flying instructors for all three Services).

Summary

6. The comparative costs for the training of Helicopter Pilots in the three Services are as follows:

Service	RN	Army	RAF
Previous FW training hours	75	40	175
Length of RW course	10 weeks	14 weeks	9 weeks
RW Aircraft used (1)	HILLER	BELL G4	SIOUX
Flying Hours (RW)	49	80	46
Number trained per annum ...	62	45	42
Cost per man trained 1972–73 ...	£9,000	£11,200	£10,400
Total Cost per annum 1972–73 ...	£557,000	£503,000	£438,000

NOTE:
1. All are light 2-seater helicopters: their running costs are roughly the same.

ANNEX F

TRAINING OF DRIVERS

Royal Navy

1. The RN employ only a small number of uniformed light vehicle drivers and these are trained by the RAF at their driving school at ST ATHAN.

Royal Marines

2. The Royal Marines train their light vehicle drivers on a 5-week course at RM POOLE. Unlike the other Services the RM course includes tuition in cross-country driving with four wheel drive vehicles and trailer towing.

3. RM POOLE also undertakes work on RM Landing Craft, special boats, ships detachment, technical training and training courses for HGV drivers and vehicle mechanics.

4. The annual cost of the RM light vehicle drivers' course is £41,800.

Army

5. Driver Training in the Army is carried out at all major units and training establishments. The costing offered for comparison is one of training, up to light vehicle standard, at the Royal Corps of Transport (RCT) ALDERSHOT. This establishment caters for the training of a variety of trades and within the RCT conducts the basic military training for recruits and in-service training courses.

6. The light vehicle training, which is part of a longer (8 weeks) course involving driving training to HGV standard, can take up to five weeks depending on the aptitude of the trainee.

7. The annual cost of training Army light vehicle drivers at ALDERSHOT is estimated to be £336,205.

RAF

8. RAF and RN drivers are trained to light vehicle standard at No. 4 School of Technical Training, (4 S of TT) RAF ST. ATHAN on a self-pacing course averaging 4 weeks 1 day. On completion of this training RAF drivers are employed on full-time driving duties in established MT driver posts. 4 S of TT conducts 75 types of courses each year in a variety of trade groups including aircraft and general engineering, mechanical transport, safety and surface, physical training, quality assurance service and some officer training.

9. The annual cost of light vehicle training of RAF drivers at St. Athan is £121,114.

Costs

10. The comparative costs for the training of light vehicle drivers are as follows:

Service & Trade	RM Drivers	Army (RCT) Drivers	RAF Drivers
Length of course	5 weeks (1)	5 weeks	4 weeks 1 day
Number trained per annum	86	1157	291
Cost per man trained 1972–73 ...	£487	£291	£416
Total Cost per annum 1972–73 ...	£41,800	£336,205	£121,114

NOTE:
1. Includes training in cross-country driving and trailer handling.

TRAINING (D.6)

Memorandum by Ministry of Defence (SCOE 31/9/2)

1. The Sub-Committee has asked for:

(a) papers on the comparative costs to each Service of the training of cooks, helicopter pilots, medical orderlies, vehicle mechanics, pay clerks, clerical staff and drivers.

(b) information on any unified training schemes showing anv savings achieved as a result of their introduction.

2. As regards paragraph 1(a), while each Service employs personnel who fall within the general categories given in paragraph 1 above, the duties vary in most cases between the Services and training is arranged to fit personnel for their particular Service task. The duties and training syllabuses for the various categories have been under examination to identify broadly analogous trades. In some cases it has been found desirable to use the cost of that part of the Serviceman's training which is comparable with training received in the other Services. In the particular case of medical orderlies it has not been possible to find sufficient similarities between the Services to carry out a meaningful cost comparison. A more detailed explanation of the trade of medical orderly is given at Annex A.

3. Because of the difficulty in identifying meaningful areas of comparison between the Services in these fields of training and of the resulting complications in the production of helpful figures of costings, the collection of information required by the Sub-Committee is necessarily taking longer than had been hoped, and therefore it will not be possible to provide the complete answers before the end of January 1974.

4. As regards paragraph 1(b), details of the unified training schemes which have been implemented are set out in Annex B.

ANNEX A

Medical Orderly

1. Although " medical orderlies " are no longer employed in the Services, all three Services employ highly skilled non-technical medical personnel trained to meet their own individual requirements.

2. There is, however, such a wide disparity between the Services in the level of training and the final qualification required to meet that need, that insufficient similarities exist to enable a useful comparison of the cost to be carried out.

3. The following definitions of the medical grades employed are provided to illustrate the basic differences between the three Services.

Royal Navy

4. The Navy employ Medical Assistants who are responsible for all the basic nursing in the Fleet and take sole charge of the medical needs of ships not carrying a medical officer. In addition to working in ships and submarines afloat they are employed in Naval Hospitals, Air Stations, RN Shore Establishments and RM Commando Units.

5. The level of medical knowledge and experience reached is up to the standard of State Enrolled Nurse, in addition to the special training required to enable the Medical Assistant to work unsupervised in small ships, submarines, and with Royal Marine Commando Units.

6. *Training*. On completion of new entry training, the Probationary Medical Assistant joins the RN Hospital, Haslar, for 22 weeks Part II Basic Medical Training. This course, which is completed by Medical Technicians as well as Medical Assistants, includes 14 weeks medical procedures; 2 weeks practical nursing; 1 week NBCD procedures and 1 week of examinations. Upon successfully completing this course, the Medical Assistant undergoes 32 weeks practical nursing in a hospital ward. At the end of this 54-week training period the Medical Assistant is qualified for advancement to Leading Medical Assistant subject to passing the final examination. Leading rate is achieved by practical experience, and if the minimum mark is not achieved at the final examination, by re-examination. Medical Assistants who specialise for duty in submarines or with RM Commando Units undergo further conversion training of between 12 and 18 weeks before joining a submarine or a RM Commando.

Army

7. The RAMC have Medical Assistants who are required to be capable of managing surgical, medical, and psychiatric patients from the outset of the condition until the patient is admitted to a hospital offering specialist medical and nursing care. He must be capable of giving the immediate first aid treatment that is necessary and carrying out the sustaining procedures required to treat a patient for a limited period in a non-hospital situation. He must be capable of undertaking the administrative procedures and documentation for patients in field units, medical reception stations and unit medical centres, including that required for and during evacuation, together with the initial documentation of patients attending hospital as out-patients or for admission. He has to be capable of performing those field and military skills required of an RAMC soldier employed as a member of any action field medical unit.

8. The RAMC Medical Assistant is normally employed in a combatant military unit, a field ambulance and a field hospital, all of which require a wide variety of training and experience in field and military skills. He can also be employed in Medical Centres, Medical Reception Stations and Military Hospitals.

9. *Training*. The RAMC soldier completes 10 weeks recruit training at the RAMC Depot and Training Centre, followed by a 4-week Medical Assistant Class 3 course at the same Depot. Upon successfully completing this course he joins the unit where for the next year he is engaged in practical work under close supervision and also receives further training in NBC and RAMC fieldcraft. At the end of this 12-month period he can, if recommended, take an upgrading examination for Medical Assistant Class 2. After a further 12-month period of employment in the category Medical Assistant Class 2 he can, again if recommended, return to the RAMC Training Centre for a 10-week upgrading course to Medical Assistant Class 1. Examinations are held before acceptance for this course and for the qualification to Medical Assistant Class 1 at the end of the course.

Royal Air Force

10. In the RAF the two distinct trades of State Enrolled Nurse and Medical Secretarial are designed to provide the medical staff necessary to cover the role of the RAF Medical Service, which is essentially to staff Medical Centres and Service Hospitals including service at isolated units without medical cover. The State Enrolled Nurse is a fully skilled nurse employed in nursing in wards and treatment rooms. The Medical Secretarial airman is primarily employed on administrative duties but is trained to first aid, elementary basic nursing, and aircraft crash duties. In Medical Centres, after normal working hours, the two trades combine to man the Medical Centre on a duty roster basis. The Medical Secretarial airman therefore requires the skill to carry out all non-medical officer duties in a Medical Centre.

11. *Training*. On completing 6 weeks recruit training the airman/airwoman joins the Institute of Health and Medical Training, RAF Hospital, Halton, for a 5-week Basic

Medical Trade Group course which includes first aid, basic nursing techniques and special safety. However, Probationary Nurses only attend a 2½-week course on first aid and special safety before joining a hospital to commence the 2-year General Nursing Council course. On completion of the 5-week Medical Trade Group Course Medical Secretarial airmen attend a 3-week Medical Secretarial Basic Course which covers documentation and office work. Those personnel selected for duty with aeromedical evacuation units, with Harrier dispersals and other specialised work attend further courses as required. Promotion to Senior Aircraftman and to Corporal is achieved after a statutory period in the Service by passing a promotion examination and by selection. Corporals attend a further 8-week course at the Institute to qualify for promotion to Sergeant.

ANNEX B

Integrated Training

1. Some unified training has been introduced over a number of years. In the majority of cases it has been implemented primarily in the interest of efficiency to provide the best possible training resources for personnel to fulfil the specific needs of each of the three Services. Considerable importance has been attached to ensuring that any rationalisation of training is cost effective, but as the prime concern has been for the Service training needs, and most of the unified training has been running for some years, any cost savings which may have occurred would now be most difficult to quantify.

2. Examples of integrated training either in part or in full are as follows:

(a) *Defence NBC School*

In 1948 the Army School of Chemical Warfare became the Joint School of Chemical Warfare (Army and RAF). The present title dates from 1964, and the School now serves the interest of all three Services.

(b) *Defence Explosive Ordnance Disposal*

The Royal Engineers and the Royal Air Force Bomb Disposal Schools amalagamated in 1959 to form the Joint Service Bomb Disposal School. In 1962 the RN School was absorbed and the amalgamation was completed in 1968 when the RN Mine Identification and Disposal Section was absorbed into the School. The instructional staff is tri-Service and the control of the School is exercised through a tri-Service committee.

(c) *Defence ADP Training Centre*

Defence ADP Training Centre was formed in 1968 at the Army School of Signals. ADP Courses had been held at the Army School since 1964 and were already available to RN and RAF personnel. However training is now formally a joint Service venture.

(d) *School of Service Intelligence/Joint Services Interrogation Wing*

Joint intelligence training officially commenced at the School of Service Intelligence in 1969; interrogation training has always been carried out on a Joint Service basis, as a separate part of the intelligence centre.

(e) *Joint School of Photography*

The Joint School of Photography was set up at RAF Cosford in 1972, resulting in the closure of the RN/Army School at RNAS Lossiemouth. Savings cannot be quantified because the Naval Air Station was transferred to the RAF at the same time, and the role of the station completely changed.

(f) *Joint School of Photographic Interpretation*

This school has been organised on a Joint Service basis since World War II.

(g) *Adventurous Training*

In 1971 the Adventurous Training Scheme was expanded throughout the three Services. In drawing up the expansion plans the opportunity was taken to share facilities on an inter-Service basis wherever this had been found to be practical and provide better value for money. In order to share the administrative task each of the three Services sponsors activities peculiar to its environment. The Army sponsors all Mountain Training, the RAF Parachuting and Gliding, and the RN Off-Shore Sailing and Sub-aqua diving. Carried out in this manner the overall cost of expanding the activities will be less than had they progressed on a single-Service basis.

(h) *Medical Training*

    Partial amalgamation has taken place in some of the more specialist areas of medical training. They are as follows:

    (i) *Dispensers*
        The initial six months training for all Services is carried out at the Army School of Dispensing, Colchester.

    (ii) *Laboratory Technicians*
        The RN and the RAF carry out the first twelve months Laboratory Technician training at RAF Halton. This arrangement began in 1967.

    (iii) *Electro-physiological Technicians*
        RAF Electro-physiological Technicians are trained at RAF Hospital Wroughton; some RN and Army personnel also attend these courses.

    (iv) *Mental Nurses*
        All student Mental Nurses are trained by the Army at the Royal Victoria Hospital, Netley. This is the only Service hospital recognised by the General Nursing Council for this purpose; both RN and Army trainees undergo a three-month secondment to Royal Naval Hospital Haslar, for the General Nursing part of their course.

    (v) *Radiographers*
        Both Army and RAF personnel receive training in Radiography at the Army School, Woolwich.

    (vi) *Radiological Protection*
        Courses in Radiological Protection are held at the Institute of Naval Medicine, Alverstoke at which personnel from all three Services attend.

TRAINING (D.7)

Memorandum by the Ministry of Defence (SCOE 31/9/2/2)

    The Sub-Committee has asked for lists of all the trade training courses offered at each of the following establishments:—

    HMS PEMBROKE, Chatham
    RCT, Aldershot
    RAPC Training Centre, Worthy Down
    RAOC Training Centre, Blackdown Barracks
    No 3 School of Technical Training, RAF Hereford
    No 4 School of Technical Training, RAF St Athan

plus similar statements for any other comparable trade training establishments.

    2. Attached at Annexes A to F are the details required for the establishments listed above. Annexes G to J contain statements for comparable training establishments as follows:—

    RM Poole, Dorset
    HQ, REME Training Centre, Arborfield
    No 1 School of Technical Training, RAF Halton
    No 2 School of Technical Training, RAF Cosford.

    3. The Sub-Committee also asked for copies of the syllabus and timetable for Cooks and Helicopter Pilots in each of the three Services. These are produced at Annexes K to M (Cooks) and Annexes N to P (Helicpoter Pilots).

ANNEX A

HMS PEMBROKE – TRADE TRAINING COURSES

RN/WRNS RATINGS (AND RM OTHER RANKS)

Basic Cook Course (RN/WRNS/RM)
Basic RN Writer (Pay/Cash)
Basic RN Writer (Sec/Admin)
Basic WRNS Writer (Pay)
Basic WRNS Writer (General – Non Touch Typist)
Basic WRNS Writer (General – Touch Typist)
Basic WRNS Writer (Shorthand)
Basic Steward (RN only – WRNS basic course at HMS DAUNTLESS)
Basic Stores Accountant (RN/WRNS)
Advancement to Leading Writer
Advancement to PO Writer
Advancement to PO Wren Writer (Pay)
Advancement to PO Wren Writer (General)
Advancement to Leading Stores Accountant (RN/WRNS)
Advancement to PO Stores Accountant (RN/WRNS)
Advancement to Leading Steward (RN/WRNS)
Advancement to PO Steward (RN/WRNS)
Advancement to Leading Cook (RN/WRNS)
Advancement to PO Cook and RM K2 and K1 (RN/WRNS)
Ships Caterer – Qualifying Course

RN/WRNS OFFICERS

Junior Supply Officers Professional Course (4th year Acting Sub-Lieutenants)
Supply Charge Course (Lieutenants (Supply))
WRNS Officers Secretarial Course (Junior WRNS Secretarial Officers)

ANNEX B

ROYAL CORPS OF TRANSPORT, ALDERSHOT – TRADE TRAINING COURSES

MANAGEMENT COURSES

Squadron Sergeant Majors
Squadron Quarter Master Sergeants
Senior MQC
Junior MQC
Potential Pilots

DRIVER TRAINING COURSES

Unit Signals Officers
Unit Signals NCOs
Driver Radio Operator Group B Class III
Driver Radio Operator Group Class III To Class II
Driver Radio Operator Group Class II to Class I
Regimental Signals Instructors
Staff Car Driver
Staff Car Driver WRAC
WRAC HGV/Ambulance
SAS Advanced Driver Training
Driver Group B Class III to Class II
Driver Group B Class II to Class I
Welbeck/RMAS

ANNEX C

RAPC TRAINING CENTRE, WORTHY DOWN, WINCHESTER – TRADE TRAINING COURSES

Long Finance and Accountancy
Cost Accountants
Service Funds Accounts (Overseas)
Service Funds Accounts (Officers and Warrant Officers)
Service Funds Accounts (Soldiers)
Transfer – In (Soldiers)
RAPC Division I
RAPC Division II
RAPC Commissioning
Transfer – In (Officers)
Unit Paymasters Advanced Training
RAPC Senior Officers
Unit Pay Duties
Regimental Services – Basic Training
Local Services
Unit Records and Pay (RAPC Division II Clerks)
Unit Records and Pay (RAPC Officers, Division I and II Clerks)
Regimental Services – Accounting
Regimental Services – Management/ADP Orientation
RAPC Automatic Data Processing (ADP)
Punch Card Operators
Clerk RAPC B1
Cost Accountants
Long Finance and Accountancy Course Entrance Examination
Institute of Cost and Work Accountants Examination – Part V
Association of Certified and Corporate Accountants Examination Section III

Clerk RAPC T&AVR Correspondence
Orientation Course T&AVR Permanent Staff
RAPC T&AVR Officers Probationary
Trade Training and Refresher, Clerk RAPC B1/B11 T&AVR
Trade Training and Refresher, Clerk RAPC B111 and NT T&AVR
T&AVR Weekend
RAPC T&AVR 11B Annual Training.

ANNEX D

RAOC TRAINING CENTRE, BLACKDOWN BARRACKS, CAMBERLEY— TRADE TRAINING COURSES

Civilian Officers
Commonwealth and Foreign Ordnance Officers
Formation Ordnance Officers
Officers Junior Management
Senior Management
Ordnance Officers
Quarter Masters—All Arms
ADP Systems Appreciation Course
Barrack Officers
Long ADP Course
Officers Food Technology
Officers Management Sciences
Officers—Provision
Officers—Unit Administration
Senior Officers—Logistics
T & AVR—Junior Officers
T & AVR Officers—Intermediate

T & AVR Officers—Visit Commanders
T & AVR Officers—Captain to Major Promotion
Warrant Officers—Pre-commissioning
Young Officers
Barrack Accountants
RQMS & CQMS All Arms
Company Quarter Master–Sergeants
RAOC WO's Senior NCOs Provision
Ammunition Technicians Regimental Training
Platoon Weapons
Recruits Basic Military Training
Recruits T & AVR
Regimental Duties Junior NCOs
  „   „   NCOs Advanced
  „   „   NCO T&AVR Refresher
T & AVR Permanent Staff Instructions

Textile Refitter B3
Textile Refitters B3 to B2
Vehicle Specialists B3
Unit Fire Officer All Arms
Bakers T & AVR
Unit Fire Officer NCOs All Arms
Bakers B3
Bakers Upgrading B3 to B2
Bakers Upgrading B2 to B1
Butchers B3
Butchers Upgrading B3 to B2
Butchers Upgrading B2 to B1
Butchers B1 Special Up dating
Butchers T & AVR
Clerks All Arms B3
Clerks All Arms T & AVR B3
Clerks All Arms T & AVR Up grading B3
   to B2
Clerks All Arms Upgrading B2 to B1
Clerks All Arms Upgrading B2 to B1
Clerks RE Upgrading B2 to B1
Clerks All Arms (Shorthand writer) A3
Clerks All Arms (Shorthand writer) A3 to A2
Clerks All Arms (Shorthand writer) A2 to A1
Clerks All Arms (Shorthand writer) A2 to A1
Clerks Technical RAOC B3
Clerks Technical RAOC B2 to B1

Clerks Technical RAOC B2 to B1
Office Management All Arms (Less APTC) *
Drivers B3
Equipment Repairers All Arms B3
Equipment Repairers T & AVR
Equipment Repairers All Arms Upgrading
   B3 to B2
Laundry Operators RAOC B3
Laundry Operators RAOC B3 to B2
Laundry Operators RAOC B2 to B1
Laundry Operators RAOC T & AVR
Printers RAOC A3
Printers RAOC A3 to A2
Printers RAOC A2 to A1
Storeman RAOC B3
Storeman REME B3
Storeman REME T & AVR
Storewoman Technical WRAC B3
Storeman REME B2 to B1
Sgt Storeman RAOC for Employment with
   Royal Sigs Units
Tailors All Arms B3
Tailors All Arms B3 to B2
Tailors All Arms B2 to B1

* Army Physical Training Corps

ANNEX E

ROYAL AIR FORCE HEREFORD
NO 3 SCHOOL OF TECHNICAL TRAINING—TRADE TRAINING COURSES

INITIAL COURSES
   Catering Officers Course Part I
   Catering Officers Course Part II
   WRAF Recruit—Reception and Initial
Training
BASIC COURSES
   Clerk Secretarial
   Steward
   Clerk Catering
   Cook (Unqualified)
   Clerk Statistics
   Clerk Accounting
   Civilian Qualified Typist/Shorthand
      Typist WRAF Basic Course
   Saudi Arabian Basic Secretarial Course
   Cook (Civil Qualified)
   Supplier II
   WRAF Admin
   Steward (SAC)
   Cook (SAC)

Steward (SAC)
   Clerk Statistics
CONVERSION TRAINING COURSES
   Telecommunications Clerk Conversion
      Course Clerical Phase
POST GRADUATE COURSE
   Clerk Secretarial (Q-SEC-T)
   Chef (Q-CAT-C)
   Clerk Secretarial (Q-SEC-S)
   Clerk Accounting (Q-SEC-NP) and
      Civilian Mess Clerk (Non-Public
      Accounting)
   Junior Catering Officers (New
      Techniques)
   Clerk Secretarial Postal Course
      (Q-SEC-P)
   Mess Managers Course (Q-CAT-MM)
   Supply Supervisors ICL 4-72 Course
   Supply Controllers ICL 4-72 Course
   WRAF Junior NCOs Training Course.

ANNEX F

ROYAL AIR FORCE ST ATHAN
NO 4 SCHOOL OF TECHNICAL TRAINING—TRADE TRAINING COURSES

BASIC COURSES
Aircraft Mechanic (Airframe)
Aircraft Mechanic (Propulsion)
Survival Equipment Fitter
MT Mechanic
MT Driver
Painter and Finisher
Parachute Packer
RAF Police/RAF Policewoman
  Driving
RAF Police Motor Cycle Course
Carpenter
Carpenter (Civilian Qualified)
General Mechanic (General Servicing
  Equipment) (GSE)
MT Driver (Army and Navy
  Personnel)
DIRECT ENTRY FITTER
General Fitter (Workshop) (WS)
Aircraft Fitter (Propulsion)
General Fitter (GSE)
FURTHER TRAINING COURSES
Aircraft Fitter (Airframe)
Aircraft Fitter (Propulsion)
MT Fitter
MT Fitter (Overseas Airmen)
General Fitter (GSE)
General Fitter (WS)
ASSIMILATION COURSES
General Fitter (Workshop) from
  Blacksmith/Welder
General Fitter (Workshop) from
  Machine Tool Setter and Operator
CONVERSION TRAINING COURSES
General Fitter
POST GRADUATE COURSES
MT Heavy Goods Vehicle Class III
  Driving (Recalled RAF Regt/
  AFDFS Personnel)
RAF Regiment Gunner Driving
  (straight through to Q-R-GDH3)
Class B Driver
Mk 6 & 6A Fire Crash Truck Driver
Crane Driving & Operating

(Q-MT-CR)
MT Fitter (Post Graduate) MT
  Management (Q-MT-MAN)
  Course
Alvis Mk 6 & 6A Fire Fighting
  Vehicle Servicing
Snow & Ice Clearance Vehicle
  (Operating)
Quality Assurance Service
Aircraft Servicing Chief Airframe &
  Engine Familiarisation
RAFVR(T) Instructor Training
  Course (Engine Phase)
RAFVR(T) Instructor Training
  Course (Airframe Phase)
Fireman Driving (Straight Through
  to Q-R-FDH2)
Fireman HGV II Driving (Recalled)
Two Piece Lathe Tools
Crane Servicing (MT Fitter)
Survival Equipment Fitter (Q-SS-FC)
POST GRADUATE COURSES
MT Electronic Test Set (Crypton)
  Operating
Driving Instructor
Oxygen Bay Servicing
Specialist Course for Mechanical
  Transport Officers
MT Heavy Goods Vehicle Class 3
  Driving (Non-RAF Regt/AFDFS
  personnel)
MT Driving Examiner (Heavy Goods
  Vehicle)
MT Driving Examiner (Refresher)
Liquid Oxygen Training for the Royal
  Navy
Oxy-Acetylene Welding Pre-Release
  Resettlement Training
Basic Fitting Pre-Release
  Resettlement Training
Car Maintenance Pre-Release
  Resettlement Training
Car Driving/Maintenance Pre-Release
  Resettlement Training

PHYSICAL TRAINING COURSE

INITIAL COURSES
Physical Education Officers Course
Pre-University Officer Cadet Scheme
Graduate Entry Scheme Outdoor
  Activities Course
BASIC COURSES
RAF Physical Training Instructor
WRAF Physical Training Instructor
RAF Regt Gunners Basic Course

Outdoor Activities Phase
WRAF Administrative
POST GRADUATE COURSES
Officials and Coaches (Non-PEdO/
  PTI)
Sports Coaches (PTI)
Flight Commanders and R & I
  Instructors Courses
Expedition Leader

ATC Outdoor Activities Course
  (Mountain Leadership Certificate
  Introductory or Assessment)
Mountain Leadership Certificate
  Introductory and Assessment
  Course
Aircrew Officers Outdoor Activities

and Survival Training
PTI Advanced Mountain Instructors
  Course
*SCFT Outdoor Activities and
  Survival Course
*Steering Committee on Flying
  Training

ANNEX G

RM POOLE—TRADE TRAINING COURSES

Driver—D1
Driver—D2
Driver—D3 basic
Driver—D3 conversion
Light Vehicle Driver—LV
Vehicle Mechanic—VM1
Vehicle Mechanic—VM2 Phase 1
Vehicle Mechanic—VM3 Phase 2
Illustrator—ILL1
Illustrator—ILL3
Metalsmith—MESM3
Armourer—Arm 1
Armourer—Arm 3
Carpenter—Carp 1
Carpenter—Carp 3

EXPLANATORY NOTES:
DRIVER TRAINING The Royal Marines

introduced the qualification of light vehicle
driver in 1973. The courses at RM Poole are
for marines who have no previous driving
experience and include basic tuition and
training in cross country driving and
trailer handling. In future the majority of
light vehicle driver training will be undertaken by units of Commando Forces RM
using unit instructors and vehicles.

VEHICLE MECHANIC TRAINING The VM3
courses are pilot courses for the new
system of training which is expected to
replace the training costed in Annex C to
SCOE 31/9/2/1. Students qualify as VM3
at the end of Phase 1 and may be selected
to continue on Phase 2 of the course to
qualify as a VM2.

ANNEX H

HQ REME TRAINING CENTRE,
ARBORFIELD, READING—TRADE TRAINING COURSES

MANAGEMENT COURSES
  Senior Management
  Junior Management (Officers)
  Junior Management (Supervisors)
  Short Management
MILITARY COURSES
  Junior REME Tactics
  LAD Commanders
  Workshop Commanders
  Regular Young Officers (Military
    Studies)
  REME Civilian Introduction
  Newly Commissioned ex-warrant
    Officers
  EME Staff Course
  REME Reserve Officers
INSTRUCTION COURSES
  Permanent Staff Instructor
  Permanent Staff Instructor
    Seminar
ELECTRONIC ENGINEERING COURSES
  Senior Officers Electronic
    Appreciation

Junior Officers Electronic
  Appreciation
Post Graduate Officers Long
  Electronic Engineering
Artificer (Radar)
Artificer (Electronic Control)
Artificer (Telecommunications)
Electronic Technician Class II to
  Class I
Basic Electronics
Technicians (Control, Radar or
  Telecomm)
Artificer (Instruments)
Instrument Technician
Electro-Medical Equipment
Equipment Repair
TRAINING BATTALION AND DEPOT REME
COURSES
Regimental Duty Qualification
Regimental—Motor Transport
  Certificate 1
Junior Regimental Duty

ANNEX I/1

RAF HALTON—NO 1 SCHOOL OF TECHNICAL TRAINING—

TRADE TRAINING COURSES

TECHNICIAN APPRENTICE COURSE
  Aircraft Technician
CRAFT APPRENTICE COURSES
  Aircraft Fitter (Propulsion)
  Aircraft Fitter (Airframe)
  General Fitter (Electrical)
  Aircraft Fitter (Weapons)
BASIC COURSES
  Aircraft Mechanic (Electrical)
  General Mechanic (Electrical)
  Aircraft Mechanic (Propulsion)
    (Overseas Airmen)
  Aircraft Mechanic (Airframe)
    (Overseas Airmen)
  Aircraft Mechanic (Weapons)
    (Overseas Airmen)
  Flight Line Mechanic (Part 1)

DIRECT ENTRY FITTER COURSES
  General Fitter (Electrical)
  Aircraft Fitter (Electrical)
FURTHER TRAINING COURSES
  Aircraft Fitter (Electrical)
  General Fitter (Electrical)
  Aircraft Fitter (Airframe) (Overseas
    Airmen)
  Aircraft Fitter (Propulsion) (Overseas
    Airmen)
  Aircraft Fitter (Weapons) (Overseas
    Airmen)
POST GRADUATE COURSES
  Aircraft Servicing Chief Instrument
    and Electrical Lead in Mk 2 "V"
    aircraft Mark 44 Torpedo Electrical
    lead in

ANNEX I/2

RAF HALTON—INSTITUTE OF HEALTH AND MEDICAL TRAINING

—TRADE TRAINING COURSES

INITIAL COURSES
  Medical Officers Initial Course
  PMRAFNS (SRN) Student Nurse
    Initial Course
  Medical Cadets Introductory Course

BASIC COURSES
  State Enrolled Nurse
  Medical Trade Group Basic Course
  Medical Secretarial
  Pupil Enrolled Nurse First Aid and
    Special Safety

FURTHER TRAINING COURSES
  Dispenser
  Operating Theatre Technician
  Medical Laboratory Technician
  Radiographer
  Electrophysiological Technician

FURTHER TRAINING COURSES
  State Registered Nurse
  Hygienist
  Physiotherapist
  Medical Secretarial

Senior Medical Officers
  Administrative Course
CONVERSION TRAINING COURSES
  Remedial Gymnast
POST GRADUATE COURSES
  First Aid Instructors
  Anti-Mosquito and Pest Control
    Units Course
  Specialist Field Nurse Course
  Audiometrician (Q-ML-AM)
  Field Hygiene and Special Safety
    Course (Q-ML-FH)
  Electrocardiograph Recordist Course
  Medical and Dental Equipment
    Training Course
  Clinical Measurement
  Permanent Commission Medical
    Officers
  Remedial Gymnast (Q-GS-RG)
  Pest Control Course for Catering
    Personnel
  Helicopter Winchman First Aid
    Course

ANNEX I/3

RAF HALTON – DENTAL TRAINING ESTABLISHMENT – TRADE TRAINING COURSES

Initial and Basic Courses
Dental Officers Initial Course
Dental Surgery Assistant
Dental Cadets Introductory Course

Technician Apprentice Course
Dental Technician
Further Training Courses
Dental Hygienist
Dental Technician

ANNEX J

RAF COSFORD – No 2 SCHOOL OF TECHNICAL TRAINING – TRADE TRAINING COURSES

Initial Courses
Signals (Overseas Officers) Course
Photography (Overseas Officers) Course (Suspended)
Air Radar (Overseas Officers) Course
Engineer (Photograph) Officers Service Application Training
Technician Apprentice Course
Electronic Technician (Air)
Craft Apprentice Courses
Electronic Fitter (Navigation Instruments)
Electronic Fitter (Air Communications)
Electronic Fitter (Air Radar)
Basic Courses
Telephonist
Teleprinter Operator
Electronic Mechanic (Air Communications)
Electronic Mechanic (Air Radar)
Electronic Mechanic (Navigation Instruments)
Electronic Mechanic (Navigation Instruments) (Overseas Airmen)
Air Photography Operator
Electronic Mechanic (Air Radar) (Overseas Airmen)
Electronic Mechanic (Air Communications) (Overseas Airmen)
Photographer (Ground) Lead-in Course
Telegraphist
Direct Entry Fitters
Electronic Fitter (Navigation Instruments)
Electronic Fitter (Air Radar)
Further Training Courses
Telephonist (SAC)
Electronic Fitter (Air Communications)
Electronic Fitter (Air Radar) (Overseas Airmen)
Electronic Fitter (Air Communications) (Overseas Airmen)

Electronic Fitter (Navigation Instruments)
Electronic Fitter (Navigation Instruments) (Overseas Airmen)
Electronic Fitter (Air Radar)

Conversion Training Courses
Air Camera Fitter
Photographic Processing Analyst
Telegraphist (From Wireless Operator)
Telegraphist (From Teleprinter Operator)
Photographer (Ground)

Post Graduate Courses
AD 470 (ARI 23146/1 & 2) First Line Servicing (Suspended)
TACAN Mk V RT 870/ARN 91 First Line Servicing for Electronic Fitters (Air Radar)
Transistor & Printed Circuit Techniques
RAFVR(T) Radio Techniques
Marconi AD 360 ADF Installation (ARI 23119) Servicing (Suspended)
Decca Navigator & Flight Log (ARI 23102 & 23121/1) Servicing
Inertial Navigation System Mk 1 & 2 (Aircraft Element))
Aircraft Camera Pack Type F49 Mk 4 (1st and 2nd Line Servicing)
Jaguar Lead-in (L techs A and L fitts NI)
Passive Warning Receivers (ARI 18223/18228) Lead-in Course
Bombing and Navigation System (QS-AV-NB)
Navigation & Bombing System (Q-AV-NB)
Lightning II Aircraft Weapons System Junior Engineering Officers Pre-employment Training
IFF/SIF/SSR – ARI 231 34/ARI 23187
ADL 21 C/A Airborne Decca Loran C & Receiver for Electronic Fitters (AC) (Suspended)

Special to Service Photographer (Ground)
Flight Instrumentation – Mk 3 Lightning Aircraft
Lightning Aircraft Instrumentation First Line Servicing (Q-AL-IFR)
Lightning Aircraft Instrument System Colour Photography

Unit Intelligence Photography
Camera Operating (Army Personnel)
F126/F135 Air Cameras Servicing
Reconnaisance Intelligence Centre Photographic Equipment Servicing
PTR 377(ARI 18220) and Automatic Test Equipment (Honeywell Titan Series 4100)

ANNEX K

COOKS TRAINING – RN/RM/WRNS COOKS – SYLLABUS

Aim: To produce a rating capable of carrying out the duties of an RN/RM/WRNS cook after completion of further on the job training.

Duration: 9 weeks. Last week for RM cook is spent at CTCRM, Lympstone.

Location: HMS PEMBROKE, Chatham.

DESCRIPTION	*Total Hours*
TRADE TRAINING	
Use of galley equipment/galley routine	$4\frac{1}{2}$
Stocks, sauces and soups	2
Fish, eggs and farinaceous	$10\frac{1}{2}$
Sweets, puddings and pastries	$7\frac{1}{2}$
Practical cookery exercises	$38\frac{1}{2}$
Butchery, meats, poultry	$18\frac{3}{4}$
Vegetables and potatoes	$10\frac{1}{2}$
Convenience Foods	$3\frac{3}{4}$
Savouries/hors d'ouvres	$3\frac{3}{4}$
Salads	$3\frac{3}{4}$
Nutrition/Dietetics/Invalid Cookery	$3\frac{3}{4}$
Breakfast dishes/packed lunches	3
Menu planning and costing	6
Use of additives	$3\frac{3}{4}$
Bakery/cakes etc	$7\frac{1}{2}$
Field Cookery	3
Hygiene	9
Written and practical tests/examinations	21
SERVICE TRAINING	
PE and Sport	30
Religious Instruction	6
Kit musters	$2\frac{1}{4}$
Current affairs	6
Cleaning Stations	12
SERVICE DIVERSIONS	
Joining and leaving procedures	$9\frac{3}{4}$
Fire and Safety Orders	$\frac{3}{4}$
TOTAL HOURS	$227\frac{1}{4}$

18 *June*, 1974.] [*Continued.*

ANNEX L

COOKS TRAINING – ARMY CATERING CORPS REGULAR SOLDIER

RECRUITS – TECHNICAL TRAINING SYLLABUS

Aim:　　To train ACC Regular Solider recruits in trade training up to the standard of Army Cook B Class III.

Duration:　　18 weeks Technical Training.

Location:　　Army School of Catering, ACC Training Centre, Aldershot.

Subject	Number of Hours (Approx) (1)		
	Lectures, demonstrations, films	Practical Cookery	Maintenance
1.　TRADE TRAINING			
Phase I (2 *weeks*) Pastry (sweets, cakes, puddings, biscuits)　...	19·5	35·25	1·5
Phase II (3 *weeks*) Butchery　...	10·5	16·5	0·75
Larder (salads, pies, fish, meat dishes) ...　...　...	21·75	33·75	1·5
Phase III (4 *weeks*) Kitchen stocks, sauces, soups, vegetables, farinaceous dishes, egg, cheese, fish and meat dishes) ...　...　...　...	27	82·5	2·25
Phase IV (2 *weeks*) Complete meal production　...　...	—	55·5	—
Phase V (2 *weeks*) Field Cookery	8·25	48·75	0·75
Phase VI (2 *weeks*) Pastry, Larder (revision)　...　...　...	0·75	56·25	0·75
Phase VII (2 *weeks*) Unit Cookery (2) ...　...　...　...	—	67·5	—
TOTAL	87·75	396	7·5
Phase VIII (1 *week*) Trade Tests		30	
2.　SERVICE TRAINING/ MISCELLANEOUS (3)			
Military Training　...　...		48	
Tests (Military Training)　...		3·75	
Games　...　...　...　...		28·5	
Physical Training　...　...		1·5	
Medical ...　...　...　...		4·5	
TOTAL		86·25	
TOTAL COURSE HOURS　...		607·5	

NOTES:

1. The course is divided into 18 weeks of 45 periods each. Each period lasts approximately 45 minutes.

2. During this phase, students work in the central kitchen preparing breakfast, dinner, tea and supper.

3. This training is carried out at various times throughout phases I to VIII.

ANNEX M

COOKS TRAINING – RAF COOKS – SYLLABUS

Aim: To teach kitchen practice, cooking methods, preparation, butchery, field cookery, hygiene, by-products, in-flight feeding, work organisation, catering equipment, portion out and stock control, catering administration and bulk cooking.

Duration: 19 weeks

Location: RAF HEREFORD

DESCRIPTION	TOTAL HOURS
TRADE TRAINING	
Administration and Organisation	8
Fundamental Elements of Cookery	14
Stocks, sauces and soups	30
Fish, eggs and farinaceous	27
Butchery, meats and poultry	90
Ancillary dishes	14
Vegetables and potatoes	30
Sweets, puddings and pastries	80
Field catering	24
Hygiene	30
Progress tests and examinations	30
Large scale catering	102
AIRMAN TRAINING	
PE and Sport	67
Padre's Hour	7
Flight safety	1
SERVICE DIVERSIONS	
Joining and leaving procedures	6
Passes	12
Wing disposal	44
TOTAL HOURS	616

ANNEX N

ROYAL NAVY HELICOPTER PILOTS – HELICOPTER BASIC FLYING TRAINING ROYAL NAVAL AIR STATION, CULDROSE

1.   DURATION OF COURSE. 10 weeks – 350 hours

2.   FLYING TRAINING SYLLABUS

	HOURS	
	DUAL	SOLO
General Handling	25.15	12.15
Navigation	3.30	—
Night Flying	2.00	2.00
Formation	2.00	2.00
TOTAL FLYING TIME	49 hours	
Total after Instructional Allowance (x 2.5)	120.00 hours	
Mass Briefings	10.00	,,
Quizzes	3.00	,,
GRAND TOTAL (Flying)	182.00	,,

3. GROUND SYLLABUS
    Principles of Flight ...   .   23.00 hours
    Communications   ...   .   15.00   ,,
    Recognition ...   .   7.00   ,,
    Navigation   ...   .   20.00   ,,
    Meteorology Revision   ...   .   2.00   ,,
    Airmanship and Safety Equipment   ...   .   15.00   ,,
    Technical   ...   .   15.00   ,,
    Supplementary Technical   ...   .   5.00   ,,
    Naval Background ...   .   9.00   ,,
    Progress Tests   ...   .   2.00   ,,
                                                                        ———
    TOTAL GROUND   ...   .   113.00   ,,
    TOTAL FLYING   ...   .   182.00   ,,
                                                                        ———
    GRAND TOTAL   ...   .   295.00   ,,
    Periods Available   ...   .   350 hours

    Difference allows for sport, station
    activities, Divisions, etc   ...   .   55 hours

ANNEX O

HELICOPTER PILOTS – HELICOPTER BASIC FLYING TRAINING CENTRE, MIDDLE WALLOP

1. DURATION OF COURSE 14 weeks – (490 hours) plus two weeks special
    attachment (See ([1]) and ([2]))

2. FLYING TRAINING SYLLABUS   HOURS
    (a) Familiarisation with aircraft   30
    (b) Preparation and After Action...   100
    (c) Flying Exercises covering: 80
                                                                (incl 28.25 Solo)

    Air Experience, Effects of Controls,
    Altitude and Power Changes, Level
    Flight Manoeuvre, Hovering, Take offs/
    landings, Circuits, Spot turns, Forced
    landings, Steep turns, Low flying,
    Night Flying, Instrument flying,
    Navigation, Emergencies
                                                                        ———
                                                        TOTAL   210 hours
3. GROUND SYLLABUS ([3])   HOURS
    (a) Principles of Flight   28
    (b) Recognition and Tactics   28
    (c) Navigation   20
    (d) Meteorology   20
    (e) Airmanship and Equipment Safety   12
    (f) Signals/Communications   28
    (g) Gunnery   58
    (h) Photography   10
    (i) Other/Tech   20
    (j) PT and Recreation   56
                                                                        ———
                                                        TOTAL   280 hours
                                                GRAND TOTAL   490 hours
NOTES:
    [1] This Basic RW course is essentially one phase of a training scheme, starting with a
Basic Fixed Wing Course and ending with an Advanced RW course (which includes such
subjects as formation flying and winching).
    [2] The course, though run at Middle Wallop, except for one week aero-medical survival
with RN and one week combat survival with SAS, is based on contract instruction by
Bristol Helicopters using Bell G4
    [3] Army students are specially selected trained soldiers and therefore do not need
military training as part of the course.

ANNEX P

ROYAL AIR FORCE HELICOPTER PILOTS – HELICOPTER BASIC FLYING
TRAINING – RAF TERN HILL, SHROPSHIRE

1.   DURATION OF COURSE (^{1}) 20 weeks (including Ground Syllabus at para 3)

2.   FLYING TRAINING SYLLABUS   HOURS
      (a) Familiarisation with aircraft   16
      (b) General Handling, hovering, landing
      forced landing, low flying, turns, navigation,
      altitude and power changes, circuits, spot
      turns, night flying, instrument flying   45
      (c) Operational handling, winching, under-
      slung loads, mountain flying, tactical
      exercises   29
                                                                    TOTAL   90 hours

3.   GROUND SYLLABUS (^{2})

   This covers principles of flight, navigation, technical subjects, safety equipment, dinghy drill, aviation medicine, meteorology, air traffic control, arrival and clearance procedures, general service training. (^{3})

NOTES:

   ^{1} This course does not correspond to the course described in Annex E to SCOE 31/9/2/1 because a new all-through Whirlwind course has since been substituted for the basic Sioux/advanced Whirlwind course of 1973. Only the basic Sioux was described in SCOE 31/9/2/1.

   ^{2} The syllabus is not broken down into parts because the RAF tries to operate on the upper part of the learning curve which requires frequent changes of programme.

   ^{3} General Service Training is given to "1st tour" officers only.

Examination of Witnesses

Mr. F. C. Herd, Assistant Under-Secretary of State (Personnel), (Defence Secretariat), Major-General J. K. I. DOUGLAS-WITHERS, C.B.E., M.C., Assistant Chief, Personnel and Logistics, Rear Admiral R. D. LYGO, Director General, Naval Manpower and Training, Air Commodore R. K. HOOKS, Director, Training (Ground), Colonel R. P. WALL, R.M., Office of the Commandant General, Royal Marines, Major-General H. R. S. PAIN, C.B., M.C., Director, Army Training, called in and examined.

Mr. *Boyden.*

1. Good afternoon, Mr. Herd and Gentlemen. Many of us are old friends, and I think nearly all of you have been here before anyway. We have had several bites at the training cherry. Could we start with the general question, what does the central staff of the Ministry of Defence, either the staff or secretariat, do about trying to get common courses by having one training course for three services or two services? In other words, what is the effort at the centre for bringing the three individual services into common ground for any training?——(Mr. *Herd.*) The effort is directed mainly through the Defence Training Committee of which ACPL is Chairman of Training, and of which I am a Member,

as are the other Director Generals, and the secretariat consist of DS15 and one of the training officers. In the past year we have taken quite a considerable initiative in examining the service requirement for training in a number of common grades, in particular the grades which your Committee has commented on, such as drivers, vehicle mechanics, cooks, helicopter pilots, and people like that. We carried on a pretty extensive study of this and three officers were employed full-time, I think for about four months, and the Defence Training Committee has studied their reports in the course of this year and come to conclusions about them. As a result of that we have commissioned certain further studies to be done, and if you wish we will put in the substance of the report of these three men as a paper.

2. That would be very helpful. Can you give us some indication of what progress has been made, and what has resulted from this study?——I think on the whole the three-man team felt the requirements in the services were genuinely different. If I may quote one example to you: take helicopters. You would think a helicopter pilot may be the same in all three services, but they are all different, and there are well-justified differences in the requirements. For instance, the RAF and RN require them to be very highly trained in instrument navigation, and then in the Army where on the whole the helicopters are cooperating in land battles the requirement for instrument training is not so great. Again, if you take a simple illustration like a pay clerk, the pay clerk in the RAF is rarely out of touch with the resources of a large pay office, for example at an RAF station. That does not apply in the Army where the pay clerk is very often operating in a small unit fairly remote from the resources of a fairly large office, for instance if you take a platoon in Northern Ireland they may be away from an office. They are trained particularly in whether they can work away from supervision when it has to be dispensed with which makes a difference to the syllabus, not a great difference but some difference. Therefore, we cannot often introduce a scheme to apply to all the services, otherwise we should be overtraining certain people, and as training is an expensive operation we have to accept for many

grades where you might think the requirement is identical it is not the same.

3. You really sound as though you are looking at it in a defensive way?——That was not the terms of their remit.

4. Can you give us some concrete examples of where the team came up with economies?——(Major-General *Douglas-Withers*.) I could not at this stage. I ought to emphasise that this three-man investigation was carried out by three officers not on MOD Staffs but by three from the single services, and full-time on the job, not in any way involved with the present staffs dealing with this policy, and they did not report until December. Therefore, the Defence Training Committee, which sits before you, and I, can tell you only what further studies the Defence Training Committee has commissioned. So there are no positive savings in pounds, shillings and pence to put before you. I should perhaps emphasise that when one looks at the scope for the basic training of various grades, which on face value appear to be exactly the same in all three services, and you yourselves have listed them and they are clearly ones which might be suitable for joint training, one finds one comes up against two difficulties, quite apart from a number of other difficulties which you consider might be emotional but which in fact in a defence policy which has taken a formal decision to retain three individual services are relevant. They are such things as the regarding of a man's training throughout his whole career n his own environment, which suffers if he is taken out of that environment and put into a joint environment occasionally. There are two reasons for this difficulty of bringing training together, and perhaps the most important is that training objectives differ. Training has become quite rightly a highly sophisticated business over the last ten years. The old days when a commanding officer decided more or less on his own training and schools thought they knew what people wanted are over. Nowadays you start from the basic objective, go out, find what you have to teach the man, go back, advise how it should be done, and go back again to make sure you are doing it right, and these are the training objectives for the three services for even simple things like cooks and drivers, and that is one of the reasons why it is difficult to bring them together. The other question is one of

18 *June*, 1974.]   Mr. F. C. HERD,   [*Continued.*
Major-General J. K. I. DOUGLAS-WITHERS, C.B.E., M.C., Rear Admiral
R. D. LYGO, Air Commodore R. K. HOOKS, Colonel R. P. WALL, R.M.,
Major-General H. R. S. PAIN, C.B., M.C.

bricks and mortar. Where you have establishments, tailor-made for the job, costing millions of pounds to build, you lose by fragmenting them and bringing them into one place, and thereby lose by building another. Having said that, the working party I have described looked into the scope for joint basic training for cooks, helicopter pilots, medical orderlies, vehicle mechanics, pay clerks, clerical staff, drivers, and spoke to members of the services' education branches and so on. At the moment a further investigation is underway involving helicopter pilots' basic training, and whether in fact there is room between the Navy and Army for the joint training of the fixed wing element of the basic helicopter course, and whether there is scope between the Navy and Royal Air Force for the support helicopter basic training of the pilots. We are examining whether we can train our medical assistants in one place. That again is an examination in depth going on now. We are examining whether vehicle mechanics can be trained in one place. Those are three examinations underway. For various reasons, which one can go into and perhaps in questioning you will want to go into, it does not make sense to train cooks, or pay clerks, or clerks, or drivers in one place.

Mr. *Boyden.*] I wonder whether we could leave the individual things until a little later. I just want to see whether the Members of the Committee want to ask any questions of what the centre is for, and then perhaps go to some of the things mentioned.

Mr. *Finsberg.*

5. Could I start by putting a question to Mr. Herd first? He knew we were investigating the training and we had some documentation. Was it really necessary for us to wait until today to hear about this three-man committee? Would it not be more in the spirit of the last report this Committee made asking for information from the MOD voluntarily, rather than hearing it in the last twenty minutes as we have today?——(Mr. *Herd.*) I apologise if we have not anticipated the wishes of the Sub-Committee in this respect. We are not really at the end of the road yet or ready to report in any specific way as the work is still in progress.

Mr. *Boyden.*

6. We want to get on to whether your method is the right one at the moment. That is the principal thing—we will go into detail in a moment—and Mr. Finsberg is saying we would have more idea of the method if you told us?——I see that.

Mr. *Finsberg.*

7. Could I ask one specific question? Was there any particular reason why this team of three officers was drawn from different services rather than the MOD headquarters?——I think there was really. We thought they might be more independent in their judgments. (Major-General *Douglas-Withers.*) I think perhaps more important the staffs of the three Director Generals of Training in our view have not got the time—I would like them to disagree if they wish—to spend enough time out in the field actually going to all the establishments concerned and looking at the training methods and syllabi, and we felt we could only do justice to the study if we invited somebody with nothing else to do.

8. Did the three officers go together, or did the Army chap always go to the Army, the Naval chap always to the Navy, and the RAF chap always to the RAF?——The answer is no, because they fragmented the work and did not do it on a colour for colour basis but very often geographically. If there were a number of establishments with different functions in a certain area perhaps one or two of the team would go to that area.

Mr. *Boyden.*

9. What rank were they?——Lieutenant-Colonels.

Major-General *d'Avigdor-Goldsmid.*

10. You appreciate what really started this was our visit to Canada. In the examination which has gone on with this three-man team has any consideration been given to what went on in Canada?—— (Mr. *Herd.*) Yes, it has, but I think the Canadian services are a little different. We still have a three services basis, whereas the Canadians are really unified in their armed services. Whilst we have the three services, Army, Navy and Air Force, I think the management of training is bound to be in single service hands. I do not mean there

will not be some joint establishments and I do not mean some single service establishments will not take on task of training people from other services as well, but I think the management is bound to be the Army, Navy and Air Force.

11. Would it not be right to say the witnesses you have here today are primarily responsible for the fighting training of their respective services and what we are dealing with is more on the "Q" side?—Indeed, the officers here today are more concerned with that.

Mr. *Boyden.*

12. Can we go to the individual services? I would like to ask this to each in turn. What conscious effort is made by, for example, the Army to see whether it can provide common training for the other services so passing its training on to the others?——(Major-General *Pain.*) Could I make a general statement before answering that, and I am not avoiding the question? This has been touched on by ACPL. My concern is not to look at this in too narrow a field. I would like to take you with me about this. If I am training a soldier in his basic trade, never forget in an era of difficult recruiting I have got to watch and see he stays with the system. Therefore, I think I would have to fight against anything which, for instance, took a cook away from his basic training unit. Major-General Douglas-Withers referred to this as whole man training, which is a way of putting it. I do not think in times of difficult recruiting that the Director of Army Recruiting, never very pleased with me anyhow because more people are lost through the initial stages of training than at any other times, would not be pleased if I took the cook away from the basic training depot or took pilots away from theirs in the early stages of training. Therefore, in looking at where I may be able to operate inter-services training I would have to exclude, and I hope you agree with me, because of the risks of wastage, that training which takes place in the first six months or so of a young recruit's career. Could you go along with that?

13. I will put it another way. Do you think it might turn out to be equal if you did get one of your cooks into the Navy? It may be a good thing for the Navy and the country as a whole, and the Navy might get someone who would prefer to be in the Navy?——I do not think, with respect, one can approach it on that basis as long as one has an Army, Navy and Air Force, and if one trained all one's vehicle mechanics in one place I suspect my Air Force colleague would be pretty apprehensive to have a young Air Force man trained for the same reason. If you had a national service or conscripted Army this would weigh very much less.

14. What I think the General has said is that you do not spend too much time thinking about this?——Certainly not during the basic training period—I do not think I dare. (Mr. *Herd.*) Our investigations into recruiting show that young men are very strongly orientated to joining the Army, Navy or Air Force and they are not very interested in the suggestion at an early stage in their career they would be transferred to one of the other services.

15. I think the Committee would take this as a major point, but we are really trying to get at a way in which whilst retaining these services you could make economies?——(Major-General *Pain.*) I think you would have to go beyond the training aspect if you were thinking of developing an all-services system. It must start in a different quarter.

16. What does the Navy do about it?——(Rear Admiral *Lygo.*) I think, broadly speaking, I take the same line as my Army colleague, for the simple reason that we know unless we get sailors into uniform and to sea quickly we will not retain them. They did not join to go into an Army establishment or even a shore naval establishment; they want to go to sea, and if they do not do so quickly we do not retain them. We are very much in line with the Army here, and we provide a naval atmosphere. If you are disciplined by the need to get the man to sea quickly this means you are bound to contain your initial training in as short a period as you can. Even in the case of cooks much of the earlier training relates to naval aspects, such as damage control, and you have to put a lot of that kind of training into their basic course. If the course were with the Army it would mean overheads or additional costs. You are not only dealing with recruits but also with instructors. One of our biggest prob-

18 *June*, 1974.]   Mr. F. C. HERD,   [*Continued.*
Major-General J. K. I. DOUGLAS-WITHERS, C.B.E., M.C., Rear Admiral
R. D. LYGO, Air Commodore R. K. HOOKS, Colonel R. P. WALL, R.M.,
Major-General H. R. S. PAIN, C.B., M.C.

lems in wastage in the Navy relates to turbulence, and we know men will not re-engage with us if we do not provide them with some stability in their careers. We know if they are ashore they expect to serve in an area of their choice more or less. If you provide naval quarters in Chatham, Rosyth and Plymouth, and so on, and then put men in an area where there is no naval connection, you would be disrupting service conditions for instructors. This is an important matter because it is their morale which rubs off on the basic recruits. We are all under the most important discipline of cost consciousness as it is, and it just so happens that in the case of cooks our throughput at HMS PEMBROKE is more or less up to capacity. It is not a simple question of our providing this elsewhere. If there were savings to be made which did not affect morale or have the spin-off of severing connections, my answer is that I would be one of the first to look at ways in which to save money, such as by putting training out to the other services. Of course, costs fall where they lie.

17. What about the RAF?——(Air Commodore *Hooks.*) We subscribe to the same philosophy as the Army and Navy. We feel it is important that the man in the early stages should identify himself with his own service. From that point we seek to identify the training he needs for the job and look for the most economic way of giving him that training. I endorse the comment by the Navy. We have no objection in principle to joint service training, but it does so happen that at the present time the most economic way of training our tradesmen is by single service training. We are maintaining close contact with the other services, and we use their courses if this is of advantage.

18. Are your training places full in the RAF?——This depends very much on the trade one looks at and the period of time. We have suffered from under-utilisation and this has been of course of our own volition. We went through stringent economy exercises which reduced the establishments at many of the units, and because we did not want to produce a major redundancy exercise it had to be through normal run-down and wastage and cutting back on recruiting, and of course this meant time. Also of course the

reduction in input to training was in many cases only temporary and, because the instructors are highly trained, and, in the case of civilians, difficult to replace on a hire and fire philosophy, we tended to maintain establishments.

19. What about the Royal Marines?—— (Colonel *Wall.*) I would go along with what the other three speakers said in relation to our particular case.

20. You might have a bias in favour of the Navy?——We are small but in our training we also adopt the concept of the whole man; we also attach considerable importance to carrying out our own command training for the same reasons as for our more specialised commando training is concerned. We are basically a non-specialist corps and we rely on the assistance given to us by other services: helicopter pilots trained by the Army, provos from the Army, cooks and so on, and we only carry out specialised training of our own where it is essential.

21. Do you have the same sort of bias for recruiting as Major-General Pain has said, where the man wants to join the Royal Marines and that is all? You do not have trouble from other services at a later stage? ——No, Sir, not on any mass scale. Obviously, from time to time we have people transfer to us, certainly from the Army and Navy; conversely, we have certainly had people transfer from us to the Navy and the Army, but on a small scale.

22. Most of your recruits want to join the Marines?——Yes, they want to be Royal Marines.

Major-General *d'Avigdor-Goldsmid.*

23. The enquiries which we made in the main dealt with initial training. Perhaps I speak for myself, but there has been a sort of inbuilt objection to this, that is to say, an objection to any form of inter-service training, and yet in your paper which you produced in January there are a number of items of integrated training. This is paragraph 2. Defence Schools, defence ordnance disposal, ADP centres, joint services intelligence, photography, photographic interpretation, are some of the points there you listed[1]. Has your committee of three come up with any positive suggestion on the items of basic trades, even one

---

[1]See pages 9-10.

of them?—(Major-General *Douglas-Withers*.) I thought I had covered this one. There is a certain amount of scope. Perhaps I could go on answering the last question and assist at the same time by seeing if I could draw the four single services' views together, as if they are speaking as Directors of their own services. There is of course a body which acts as a catalyst for looking into the scope for rationalisation. Since moving into one building the MOD has the policy that the services should rationalise where it is cheaper and at least as efficient. That policy is there and it has been pursued with a great deal of success, largely in the logistic field. We are not discussing that, but also in the other fields we have scope for there has been success. So we are under constant remit in the Defence Training Committee to look at things for rationalisation. Our success story is limited not because anybody is fighting against the policy but because it is beyond our imagination to match up the evaluation of things to the major criteria that it is cheaper and at least as good. Therefore, when we gather in the Defence Training Committee to consider these trades and disciplines it is with an absolutely open mind, and we genuinely try to rationalise according to our remit. I hope I can get that message across fairly, because it is utterly so.

24. How did the approaches for rationalisation come up?——Because we know it is the policy to rationalise we look at our trades. Largely it is my job to start the ball rolling. We look to see where we might have scope and examine it.

25. Do you know the cost comparisons of training similar people in different services?——We do indeed. It is not of course at our finger tips, but it could be produced if required.

26. Could you tell us what it costs to train as a Navy, Army or Air Force cook? ——Yes, I can tell you in that particular instance. Taking last year as a yardstick, the Army and Navy prices were relatively the same and the Air Force was more expensive. There was a good reason because the Air Force had more expensive overheads in an establishment running down. We can tell you in certain cases. You might be able to produce ones I could not tell you.

Mr. *Boyden*.] Does any other Member of the Committee wish to ask questions on this single service rationalisation aspect?

Mr. *Finsberg*.

27. Yes, Chairman. This goes back to what the General said in his opening remarks where he was saying why certain things could not be done. Could he explain where on rationalisation, for example, consideration has been given to laying down the basic syllabus for a particular operation, whether it be pay clerks, helicopter pilots and so on, and then once that is done over and above that the individual service would complete it? The RAF and Army would find they would want extra weeks for navigation and the training of pay clerks. Where is the basic rationalisation of the syllabus?——When we examine the scope for rationalisation we have to examine it under such headings as trade objectives, costs, real establishment and manpower morale. Leaving out the last factor for the moment, we look to see whether we can gain something by having a basic syllabus as opposed to losing something, which would mean every service would probably have to change their training objectives for the basic training in order to meet in the middle. That is one of the factors we have to consider. If that were to be, provided it was more effective and cheaper, there would be no question but it would be done.

28. Has the MOD done a detailed study of one trade, irrespective of what it is, on a rationalisation basis to see whether it could be done, to have a basic syllabus and leave the individual four services to build up their specific requirements on that?—— Yes. The Defence Training Committee has after all examined most of these things several times. This is a continuing process, and specifically the three-man committee I mentioned did examine this very thing and they reached an impartial conclusion on it. (Mr. *Herd*.) Could I add to this? When you get these syllabi they are scrutinised financially to see if any aspects can be eliminated as unnecessary for the task the trainee has to perform in his own service. So to some extent I am bound to admit this financial pressure does tend to work against the common syllabus because we wish to eliminate any unnecessary training.

29. Could we move on to specific examples? I have figures for cooks in front of me which show the costs of successful students in the different services: an RAF/WRAF cook costs roughly £1,200, a WRAC cook costs £424, an Army cook £606, and the Marines and Navy cooks are very much cheaper at roughly £300. The question to the layman is this extraordinary difference in the costs. Does it not provoke you into trying to foist the Navy's cheaper method on the RAF?——The Army course, of course, is twice as long as that of the Navy or Royal Marines, the Navy and Royal Marines courses being nine weeks as opposed to the eighteen weeks for the Army.

Major-General d'Avigdor-Goldsmid.

30. Do they not eat in the same manner?——(Major-General *Pain*.) No, they do not. I have a ready-made example on hand in Northern Ireland. An Army cook has to be capable of completing without supervision a meal we would all like to eat. In many camps and barracks he is under supervision, but he has to be capable of performing on his own feet and that is probably why we go for a longer period.

Mr. Boyden.

31. On those standards the RAF must have terrible difficulties in feeding people?——(Mr. *Herd*.) The difficulties arise because in 1972/73 they had small courses going through the establishments and so they were under-utilised.

Major-General d'Avigdor-Goldsmid.

32. Have you not put your thumb right on what we are trying to get at?——I realise that is what you are trying to get at, but the RAF figures are wholly misleading in the sense that they relate to 1972/73 when the courses were quite exceptionally distorted and small. However, the comparison between the Army and the Royal Navy does bring out this point of different requirements.

Mr. Finsberg.

33. Major-General Pain has just said the Army need to have men who can cook unsupervised under any conditions. In that case why is it the Army course only allows about 56 hours for sweets and puddings while the RAF allows 80 hours?——(Major-General *Pain*.) I must take a certain amount of defence in the size of the training organisation. This goes into the technical aspect of how many hours you require to train a chap in preparing sweets and things. I must get advice from the Director of the Army Catering Corps. A lot of his work is not known in detail to my Directorate.

34. Does it not seem a complete contradiction from what he said earlier? The Army requires men to do the cooking in an unsupervised way away from anywhere or anyone and yet only just over half the time is allowed for the preparation of sweets compared with the RAF?——(Air Commodore *Hooks*.) I think the figure is a little misleading. I think if one breaks the syllabus down and brings all the similar things together, the figures are about 80 for the RAF and 83 for the Army for that subject.

Mr. Boyden.

35. How would you react to the introduction of a civil cook and letting him roam round and find out about economies and improvements and so on?——(Major-General *Pain*.) I do not think we are adverse to anything which would make large savings, if there are large savings to be made, and we would make cuts. I must always come back to the point I made earlier. We do not even recruit to the Army, as indeed you know, but we recruit to regiments and corps—we do not sell the Army. The question of bringing up a cook in his own regiment is very strong and during that training he is doing other training as well.

36. I remember to this day how good the young men in the Army Catering Corps were at other things?——The Army Catering Corps is one of the biggest success stories in recent years. Some of the cooking when we were young was not all that hot, but since the 1960s it has done very well.

37. I do not see why if you had somebody looking at the whole field of cooking and that sort of thing you might not come up with some considerable economies not affecting this at all?——(Major-General *Douglas-Withers*.) There is considerable liaison between the services and the service schools. They are looking at each other's methods in detail to see if there is something one has that the other can profit from.

Mr. *Finsberg.*

38. Could I refer to document D7, SCOE 31/9/2/2? Annex L shows in great detail the cooks' training with the Army Catering Corps and Annex M shows "Cooks Training—RAF Cooks—Syllabus", and the figures I extracted earlier came from that. If we are told by the RAF those figures are not right presumably somebody accepted responsibility for putting this memorandum in. Perhaps we might know why the Army's time is not correct, and we are also told the RAF's time is not accurate?——(Air Commodore *Hooks.*) The figures are correct. I am afraid I misled you. It is just that the headings are slightly different, and they cover slightly different content. For example, there is " Pastry (sweets, cakes, puddings, biscuits) " for the Army and further down " (2 weeks) Pastry, Larder (revision) " 56.25 hours. The figures I referred to were trying to gather from that detail the time compared with the RAF.

39. Perhaps I could ask Mr. Herd or Major-General Douglas-Withers just to clear it up. Is it fair to say that any of the figures in this memorandum are on a like for like basis or are they all different? Do you see my point?——(Mr. *Herd.*) I see your point. In the time available, which was about a week, we had to produce this memorandum and we thought we had it right. I think these figures are still fairly reliable. It might be there is some discrepancy in them. I would like an opportunity to go through them more carefully but, as I understand it, these are not misleading.

40. It may be the headings are misleading?——Maybe they are.

Major-General *d'Avigdor-Goldsmid.*

41. Could I ask a question on the accommodation side? I know the Omar barracks at Aldershot, and the Navy are at Chatham and the RAF at Hereford. Is any of these three establishments big enough or could it be made big enough without an enormous rebuild to carry out the initial training of all three services?——Unfortunately, they are not big enough at the moment to take all three services; indeed, in none of the fields are we able to find one establishment that could take on the task.

If it could the pressure would be enormous to make some move in that direction. This is not to say the situation will remain like that indefinitely. One does not know what will happen as a result of the defence review. That is the situation at the moment. We are particularly looking at this problem in the case of cooks to see whether any of the establishments could take all the cooks for all three services, but it is not possible at present.

42. Has any estimate been made of what it would cost to enlarge one of the three in order to do this?——No, it has not, Sir. Quite frankly, I am sceptical whether anyone would be willing to give us any money for building at the present time. The atmosphere in the services is not one which is very favourable to any proposals for new buildings at the present time.

Mr. *Boyden.*

43. If we are to accept the argument you must train the new recruits in each service, that does not have the same force when you are giving advanced courses for NCOs and so on, or does it?——(Major-General *Pain.*) I see it could not or need not, it is quite true. It is important in the early stages. Once you have set up an establishment to do the bulk of the training, which is your recruit training, for the numbers concerned it is probably most economic to do the advanced training in the same place. I would not object to the common advanced training of cooks but it is probably more economic to do it in the same spot.

44. Perhaps one of you could give an example of the volume of training, accepting the General's idea that you must have your recruits and training in the same service?——(Mr. *Herd.*) We get to the definition of the services: the services exist virtually for training in peace time.

45. Where could we have this where Army morale would not be affected by mixing up with sailors?——(Major-General *Pain.*) I could not give any figures. I think it would be quite acceptable to train your Army cooks, B1 tradesmen, the top class of cook, at the same establishment, but the numbers would be so small perhaps you would wonder whether it would be cost effective.

46. I would have thought at that stage there would be some morale advantages in having the services together?——(Mr. *Herd.*) There might indeed. I would like to consider that question.

47. Perhaps you could give us a note on this field of advanced cooking or anything else which would warrant looking at?—— (Rear Admiral *Lygo.*) I think we have to come back to the point of the conditions of service. You have to accept the fact you have to provide the right environment for a chap to serve for long periods. I have expressed a view of turbulence already. If you are going to send him off to some totally foreign part of the country, you have upset his terms of service to some extent. (Major-General *Pain.*) This applies to some degree to the Army though in a slightly different context. I should never support the view of doing part of a course in one place and then part somewhere else. If this is a job where he can bring his wife, and then you have this turbulence because part of it is in A and part in B.

Major-General d'*Avigdor-Goldsmid.*

48. You have already mentioned the disparity between 9 weeks and 19 weeks. Is that figure of 16 weeks such a bedevilment of the sailors' desire to go to sea?—— (Rear Admiral *Lygo.*) At the present time in certain categories we are down to $5\frac{1}{2}$ months between sea service. Therefore, taking 16 weeks out of that $5\frac{1}{2}$ months to that man is a very large chunk indeed.

49. At the present time you are taking 9 weeks out of it?——He is going into an area where he is already identified as a cook. He might reasonably expect that the time he has ashore should be in the Chatham area and, therefore, it is reasonable for the man to obtain a house or married quarters or council house in Chatham or such an area. If you send him off to Scotland for six weeks' training he will not take to it kindly.

50. If you take it to the Army . . .?—— (Major-General *Pain.*) I was only less unhappy about the advanced training, provided it did not involve turbulence to families in that course.

Mr. *Boyden.*] But you would be prepared for a little turbulence in this way.

Major-General d'*Avigdor-Goldsmid.*

51. The point I was making was in relation to the initial training when one hopes the chap is not married?——(Rear Admiral *Lygo.*) I thought we had moved on to advanced training.

Mr. *Boyden.*] Is there anything else on cooks?

Mr. *Finsberg.*

52. Could I ask Mr. Herd a very simple question? How is it possible for MOD to make any meaningful estimates as to whether joint courses or three or four separate courses are financially correct if they do not start off at MOD with clearly defined definitions of trade?——(Mr. *Herd.*) I thought I said, Sir, the training requirement varied between the services, we think justly. The requirements for training for people whose names are the same, such as cooks, does vary between the services, and it is not wrong because the requirements are different.

53. Perhaps I did not phrase my question very well. If we stay with cooks for the moment, in the document you have sent us, which I put to you you could not have prepared specially for us—?——We prepared this specially for you.

54. —you have never tried to work out how many hours are spent in the four services for sweets, puddings and pastries? ——This information has been available, but the documents were prepared especially for you.

55. If the information is available in order to get a proper like for like cost per annum, do you not need to say the training for making " afters " takes X number of hours whether by Navy, Army, Marines, or Air Force? What I am saying is that the documentation you have given us does not convey that simple figure because we might have to extrapolate certain items, but you have such figures at the MOD?——(Major-General *Douglas-Withers.*) We have not got it, and the Army did not pluck a figure of so many hours out of the air, nor did the Navy or Air Force. According to what time they have available in a soldier's career for training they cast up the syllabi, and they do not decide that X is the only number of hours for cooks to be trained, and I see no savings from it.

Mr. *Roper.*

56. Could the RAF give us some evidence on this? According to Annex A of document D1, we are told one of the reasons their figures are high is because they had a lower level of training, but they have also done a job analysis and reduced the length of the course from 19 weeks to 14 weeks?——(Air Commodore *Hooks.*) This was based on defining what a man needed to know after leaving training. We would analyse what was taught to the cook. He was taught butchering and in-flight feeding in more detail than he needed, and so we reduced that and the course length from 19 weeks to 14 weeks. If a limited number of people needed this particular training we would teach it at a later stage, but we found the average cook did not need this knowledge.

57. Could this system of job analysis not be provided elsewhere and end up with providing a more common syllabus?——It tends to be subjective in the end, how many hours a cook needs for a certain subject.

Mr. *Boyden.*

58. Do you do it in other contexts?—— Yes.

59. And the other services?——(Mr. *Herd.*) Yes.

60. Can you give us other results in the field of training?——(Rear-Admiral *Lygo.*) We have introduced a system called CODAP, an objective method that records job analysis. We have found that in the training of two of our sub-specialist electrical mechanics certain parts of the course were common and, therefore, we have readjusted training in HMS Collingwood to avoid duplication. We are about to extend it to the whole of the engineering branch of the Navy. There is a questionnaire in which we identify to what extent the man trained uses the skills learnt. We use this information to refine the training course and cut out the unnecessary parts, always bearing in mind it is not absolute but an indication of where to make improvements. (Major-General *Pain.*) We have recently set up the Army school of instructional technology at Beaconsfield, and we have advisers who have been through the course of system training using objectives and analysis; it incorporates the use of simulators and closed-circuit tele-

vision. There are many strides being made and we have gone a long way towards modern, easy methods. The Army manual is so thick and consists of many different trades, and I must admit I am concentrating on trying to get this working through my own system, with cooks and others. There has been consultation between the various directors, who doubtless are comparing the syllabi and objectives with each other, but it takes a long time to work it out.

Mr. *Finsberg.*

61. Referring to this annex, Annex K, the Navy allocated 9 hours for hygiene, the RAF 30, and the Army do not appear to allocate any. Surely, hygiene is something which would be common to all services. Could I ask why there should be that amount of difference between the RAF and Navy, and where the Army do their hygiene with the unsupported man away from his modern cooking facilities and instruction? ——(Major-General *Douglas-Withers.*) At the bottom of the page of Annex L there is 4·5 hours.

62. Does Mr. Herd now see the problem. It is impossible to get any sensible comparisons from these documents?—— (Mr. *Herd.*) We were asked to produce this at a week's notice. I am sorry about this. We had very little time to go through these and make sure there were no inconsistencies. There may be some discrepancy in the terminology in cases, but I am fairly confident there are no errors in the facts themselves. It may be difficult to make comparisons because different terminology may be applied in different services.

Mr. *Boyden.*

63. I wonder if we could go through different areas; for example, with regard to clerical staff one of the basic questions there seems to me to be do the three services try and rationalise some of their clerical procedures, doing all similar things, so the training might be common?—— Yes, I think some effort is made. Again, the clerks' tools of the trade in the different services are somewhat different, the forms and clerical processes. What the clerk in Army job has to know about will vary considerably from the forms and clerical processes in the Navy which the clerk there would have to make himself familiar with,

and again that would vary from the terminology and forms used in the RAF.

64. To take an area which is common, like personnel matters, leave and that sort of thing, are the forms used and methods used different—I suspect they are?——Yes, the terminology is different and the description of trade is different. Very often in the three services there is not a common terminology through the three services at all.

65. I thought there was a big effort made some years ago to get common Queen's Regulations?——They are being evolved, which takes quite a long time.

66. Is not the law in common with the services now?——Yes, to some extent but not absolutely exactly the same. The main effort in this field in the past has been devoted to getting services personnel documents and pay documents and so on rationalised on a single service basis, and from that we have got considerable savings by identifying the paying documents with the personnel administrative documents, and by using the computer we have made considerable savings in the three single services, but this has been done in a single service not across the services. That has been the main effort in the last few years.

67. Could you give us an example in which service is there a basic one for one thing and which has the one in another?——I think I had better put in a little note on that, and of the savings we have made as a result of doing this.

68. You have been rationalising the clerical procedures by making one service common to the other two?——No, Sir. I must have expressed myself badly. What we have done is to rationalise the pay documents and personnel administrative documents for one service, that is to say, the Navy, Army and RAF. The pay documents and personnel administrative documents have been rationalised on a single-service basis not a tri-service.

69. Is there scope for making it tri-service?——I do not know that there is a great deal of scope.

70. Not for a common thing like pay, for example?——Not really. The terminology in the services is so different. We are going to look at that, and we have the pay

and services record working party which is beginning to grapple with this, but it will be a long and difficult job I am afraid.

Mr. *Finsberg.*

71. Is the working party drawn from three services, or have you tried to get an independent body to look at it?——They are just drawn from within the MOD.

72. Have you considered asking the civil service to do this for you?——I am sure we have, and I do not know whether they should be able to contribute very much to this. It is a question of sorting out the documentation in the MOD.

73. Have you considered the advantage of having an outside body like the civil service who are not slowed down by thinking of different terminology?——I have not considered it. Maybe my predecessors have done.

74. Could we have a note to see whether it has been actively considered?——(Major-General *Douglas-Withers*.) All the pay in the services is done on a single-service basis by computer. A decision has been taken for reasons of economy not to try and bring the three service personnel computers on an interface. Another decision has been taken, because savings can be shown, to bring logistic computers on interface. Because the service personnel computers will remain independent, which is inevitable with the pay requirements being different in the three services. I am not sure there would be very much to gain in bringing in an independent civil service body to examine the three pay systems.

Mr. *Boyden.*

75. Shall we move on from clerical staff and pay to vehicle mechanics?——We are examining the possibility of training all the vehicle mechanics at Bordon. (Mr. *Herd*.) The Army will then do all the services.

76. Could you give a general argument for and against that at the moment?——(Major-General *Douglas-Withers*.) If I could have just a moment? (Mr. *Herd*). The argument for is that the similarity in the requirements for the mechanic in the three services may be sufficiently close to one another to make it possible to train them all in a single unit, which I think is the point the Sub-Committee are anxious to

18 *June*, 1974.]   Mr. F. C. HERD,   [*Continued.*
Major-General J. K. I. DOUGLAS-WITHERS, C.B.E., M.C., Rear Admiral
R. D. LYGO, Air Commodore R. K. HOOKS, Colonel R. P. WALL, R.M.,
Major-General H. R. S. PAIN, C.B., M.C.

come to. (Major-General *Douglas-Withers.*) If I could read out what the Defence Training Committee said: " The three-man report established that the school of electrical and mechanical engineering had the capacity and ability to devise tailor made courses for the RM and RAF vehicle mechanics to suit single service training objectives and the Army would investigate on behalf of the RM, Army and RAF the possibility, costs, advantages and disadvantages of colocating all vehicle mechanic training at SEME Bordon ". (Major-General *Pain.*) And we are trying to cost this now.

Major-General *d'Avigdor-Goldsmid.*

77. Is there some reason why the Navy have civilian mechanics?——(Rear Admiral *Lygo.*) We do not drive vehicles at sea. We only support the training necessary for going to sea. Anything we do not have to do at sea we civilianise. The supporting services for the Navy are to a large extent civilianised in general as opposed to the other services.

Mr. *Finsberg.*

78. How do the Marines fit in?——(Colonel *Wall.*) At the moment we are training our own vehicle mechanics except when we wish them to have higher skills and then they are trained by the Army.

Mr. *Boyden.*

79. What about drivers? It seems to me we have had a preliminary skirmish in this field where rationalisation might be economic. Could you give us an indication of what your three-man team is thinking on that?——(Major-General *Douglas-Withers.*) Perhaps you would not like me to read, I do not know, but they took note that the basic requirement was 10,000 a year for basic training, and over half of those are trained at two places Aldershot and St. Athan. Already the RAF trains 280 Royal Navy trainees—I think the full requirement—and Army trainees to the extent of 300 each year, and the factors which militate against going further are, first of all, the construction of a new, bigger establishment where 10,000 would be under training, which costs millions of pounds and does not exist, and the environmental factor. The people at Aldershot put up with the Army as they have done all their lives, but if you

move to Birmingham or somewhere else you make it unacceptable to civilians.——(Mr. *Herd.*) There is also a limit on the given number of drivers in an area, because it eventually becomes intolerable for the people in the area.

Mr. *Finsberg.*

80. When we saw your predecessors in 1972 they were concerned with training drivers by civil contract, question 651, 14th March, 1972?[1]——(Major-General *Douglas Withers.*) It was turned down. Nobody except The British School of Motoring was in a position to train, and it was thought intolerable to put it into the hands of one big firm and give it the monopoly. It was also thought to be more expensive and less reliable.

81. As the Ministry were considering it, why could nobody have the courtesy to tell the Committee why it was turned down? Could it not have come in the form of a paper or something?——I apologise. Sir James Dunnett himself accepted the arguments were valid, but of course you must see the arguments.

Mr. *Boyden.*

82. What is the wastage rate of drivers in the three services? Is there any scope for looking at wastage rates and seeing whether any improvements are required in the training?——Do you mean the wastage rate by their not having aptitude?

83. Yes, the failure rate?——Yes, we will answer this question.

84. Could you let us know? Let us move on to helicopter pilots. We have had a fair amount to do with helicopter pilot training. Do you have any views on how this is moving, whether there is any rationalisation taking place here?——(Mr. *Herd.*) Certain facets of helicopter training I think one could look at. However, Major-General Douglas-Withers did mention that the Defence Training Committee did commission studies into further rationalisation of certain aspects. (Major-General *Douglas-Withers.*) The RN is to undertake an investigation in the Navy and Army into fixed wing, and the Navy is to undertake an investigation in the Navy and RAF on support helicopter training and Royal Marines training.

[1]Ninth Report from the Expenditure Committee HC (1971-72) 516-II.

Mr. *Roper.*

85. In D7, Annex P 3(2), it says; " The syllabus is not broken down into parts because the RAF tries to operate on the upper part of the learning curve which requires frequent changes of programme." I wonder if Air Commodore Hooks could help us with that?——(Air Commodore *Hooks.*) This was not familiar to me too, so I enquired to find out what it meant. It means we try to make the best use of training time. For example, if it were raining and we could not fly we would move part of the training period to something which could be studied inside.

Mr. *Roper.*] Do you think the documents in future could not attempt to baffle us with science?

Mr. *Boyden.*

86. All helicopter pilots already have their wings before they fly helicopters in the RAF?——Yes.

87. Do they go again to fixed wing flying or do they end up as helicopter pilots? ——They can go back to fixed wing in the distant future, although they would be regarded as helicopter pilots immediately after training.

88. How long would be the period?—— This would depend on the pilot.

89. What would be the average time? ——Normally they would stay on helicopters for the effective part of their flying career. A pilot could leave flying for a while and then go back to flying as a station commander maybe, but he would not be a full-time operational pilot, although he would be qualified.

90. They would normally be helicopter pilots unless they went out on some other limb?——Yes. We would seek to get the most profit from the training by keeping them on helicopters for many years.

91. It means the RAF pilots for helicopters have much more training than any other pilots?——Up to a point. I think the Army might have some comments to make. (Major-General *Douglas-Withers.*) In terms of hours, the Navy have 75 hours of fixed wing training before they go on to helicopter training. The RAF have 30 hours of simple fixed wing training and 145 hours on jets. This is much more, but they want to have flexibility in the Royal Air Force for moving pilots from fixed wing to rotary, although they do not do it that much. The Army take 40 hours on basic fixed wing flying.

92. Is this for emergency situations in which RAF pilots would be drafted from helicopter pilots back to their original role?——(Air Commodore *Hooks.*) The reason we do a fair amount of the fast fixed wing flying is because it can be very difficult to select pilots with the aptitude for the most critical area of jet stream and, therefore, we have to make sure the pilots for fighters and jet aircraft are the ones with the most aptitude and we do not miss potential by streaming them too early.

93. Does this mean there is a limited number in the population where you can only get the numbers you want?——I think we get the numbers we want. If there were a number with an aptitude for fast jet streaming, we would like to look at them all before deciding which ones went into the fast jet stream, which the multi-engine and which the helicopter streams.

Mr. *Finsberg.*

94. The highest cost for training men is in the Army where they are trained by Bristow Helicopters. Is there any reason why, as it appears to be the most expensive way of training the men, it is not handed over to the RAF?——(Mr. *Herd.*) I think one would expect the longer course to reflect the higher cost.

95. In that case I will reverse my question. Would it not be cheaper for everybody else to have their training done by Bristow Helicopters? —— (Major-General *Pain.*) Bristow Helicopters provide the instructors, and the machines are ours. This is rather like sub-contracting the task of training to Bristow. I have been down there and seen them. You get these very experienced chaps who are civilians employed by Bristow, and you find the stability fairly essential in basic flying. It is a pretty hair-raising business I imagine, and I think the people we have from Bristows have proved to be extremely competent.

96. Would the RAF or Army not feel it was a better way of doing it?——(Rear-Admiral *Lygo.*) You are talking about a total cost difference of something like

£50,000, Sir. If you add up the hours, the total flying hours of the Army and Navy are very similar, 120 hours to 124 hours. We are talking about a difference in cost per man of £2,000, but it is difficult to compare for the reasons we have expressed, the content of the courses is different. If you were to increase the fixed wing element of Army training, an expensive element, you would push up the price for Royal Navy training over all for what we think is required to have safe pilots in the fleet. We would have to think again about having fixed wing pilots.

97. Have the Navy considered Bristows?——Yes, we have. We have used civil training for fixed wing pilots and we did it by contract.

Mr. *Roper*.

98. If you go back to the previous page you will see the figure for the Navy is £9,000 for the rotary wing course in 1972–73, whereas the Army cost was £11,200 for both the fixed and rotary wing course?—— I was assuming they were the same but they appear to be not.

Mr. *Boyden*.

99. Do you know the answer to that, Mr. Herd?——(Mr. *Herd*.) I do not know the answer when they are not comparable, but they are as comparable as we can make them given the different courses.

Mr. *Roper*.

100. With respect, I think the Rear Admiral would agree a certain amount of the arguments falls?——(Rear-Admiral *Lygo*.) I accept this is the case. We are now coming back to comparing the price of the helicopters. There is a difference between the cost of the Hillers, which the Navy has, and the Bells, which the Army has, and I think there might be a relatively small difference between the two figures.

101. We are told the running costs are the same. It may be a difference in the cost of doing it yourself rather than Bristows doing the instructing?——It could be found if it were broken down in detail.

Mr. *Finsberg*.

102. Would it not have been broken down in detail if the exercise showed it was not to be done on a single-service basis? Are they like for like or not?——(Mr.

Herd.) They are as near like for like as we can make them.

Dr. *Miller*.] Referring to the previous question about total costs and training helicopter pilots, I think you yourself put your finger on one piece of information we would have to have before giving an answer, that is wastage. It may be that in one or more of the services there is a much higher wastage for a variety of reasons. It may be that the Army has a very much greater potential intake and, therefore, would have a much higher failure rate. This is a piece of information we could want.

Mr. *Boyden*.

103. Shall we move on to the medical field? We discussed it recently when we met Sir Clifford Jarrett. Has any more been done on that aspect?——(Major-General *Douglas-Withers*.) The Defence Medical Services Co-ordinating Committee have accepted in principle that medical orderlies will be trained in one place. They are now deciding when and how.

104. What about the dental hygienist? We have one or two fields in which the Jarrett Committee made recommendations and we pushed a little harder, for example, unification of training of dental hygienists? ——(Mr. *Herd*.) I think the answer to that one is that the Jarrett Committee recommended that the dental hygienists' and dental technicians' training should be done by RAF Halton. I think the difficulty with this is that the two grades need a considerable amount of practical work if they are to be trained properly, and it is doubtful whether the number of people available to Halton will enable them to be trained practically for this job.

Mr. *Finsberg*.

105. What about the radiographers? ——Again, the decision has been taken in principle. It is feasible to train them in one place, and the services are deciding where it should be done and are consulting.

Dr. *Miller*.] I commend the services on breaking down the medical and dental services. Looking at it there are as many difficulties with inter-service training of medical assistants as there are with other grades in the forces. If one thinks, for example, of the different ways in which accidents are caused, it is very often important to have the cause of the accident to know how to treat it effectively. If the services can get hold of that one and get over it, there is no reason why they should not be able to get over other problems we have been discussing today.

Mr. *Boyden.*

106. What about laboratory technicians? The Jarrett Committee said they were trained by each service in small numbers and recommended inter-service training? —— (Major-General *Douglas-Withers*.) I think I misled you. I said on medical orderlies a decision has been taken. I think I should have said a decision has been taken on laboratory technicians, radiographers, and physiotherapists, and not on medical orderlies.

Mr. *Boyden*.] Perhaps you could give us a note on the medical field?

Mr. *Finsberg.*

107. With regard to male nurses, are they orderlies or something completely separate?——(Mr. *Herd*.) We did put in a note saying the term "medical orderly" meant different things in different services.

108. The General has just used it, and that is why I asked?——The term "medical orderly" means such different things in the three services we could not make a genuine comparison. The integrated programme is for physiotherapists, radiographers, and laboratory technicians, and these are the people we are aiming to train at one place.

109. Are you expanding or improving the training of male nurses following the recommendations of the Jarrett Committee? Would it not be a chance for unifying their training at a higher level? ——I recollect that the Jarrett Committee recommended it. I cannot say off-hand exactly what the position is. If you would like a note on that, I will give you a note again.

Mr. *Boyden*.] We thought the development rather slow on the Jarrett Committee Report, but we would like to be brought up to date.

Mr. *Finsberg.*

110. The Jarrett Committee did in fact talk about career prospects for male nurses being improved. This might have been something on which action would have been taken after twelve months?—— (Major-General *Pain*.) I think I have heard there might be an opportunity of commissioning a certain number of male nurses. (Mr. *Herd*.) I think this has to be considered in conjunction with recommendations about nursing services in general. I think it is by no means easy to take one of the Jarrett recommendations in the nursing context and implement it by itself. There are a series of recommendations about the nursing services, if I am right, which we have to take as a whole.

Mr. *Boyden*.] We have gone into great detail with some of the things, but we do thank you for attending and giving evidence in such detail. Thank you very much, Gentlemen.

MINUTES OF EVIDENCE TAKEN BEFORE THE EXPENDITURE COMMITTEE (DEFENCE AND EXTERNAL AFFAIRS SUB-COMMITTEE)

SESSION 1974-75

MINUTES OF EVIDENCE TAKEN BEFORE THE
EXPENDITURE COMMITTEE (DEFENCE AND
EXTERNAL AFFAIRS SUB-COMMITTEE)

TUESDAY, 10TH DECEMBER, 1974

Members present:

Colonel Sir Harwood Harrison, in the Chair

Sir Frederic Bennett	Mr. Anthony Kershaw
Mr. James Boyden	Dr. Maurice Miller
Mr. Bernard Conlan	Mr. John Roper
Mr. Geoffrey Finsberg	Mr. Neville Sandelson

RAF ORGANISATION REVIEW—RAF MANPOWER
ECONOMIES (D.16)

Memorandum by the Ministry of Defence (SCOE 69)

Timetable and Progress to Date

1. Since the inception of the RAF Manpower Economy Project in 1971, 5,872 Service and 1,471 civilian posts have been given up. The exercise is a continuing one and further economies on a declining scale are expected to accrue in future years. However, future savings are of course likely to be affected by decisions arising from the current Defence Review.

Evaluation of the Savings

2. The manpower savings are, in general, recurrent savings. The annual value of the posts already eliminated, costed at standard capitation rates, amounts to about £18·5 million.

Capital Expenditure Involved

3. The capital expenditure necessary to secure the manpower economies has been relatively small since most have been achieved within the framework of existing facilities. Preparation of a complete list of all capital outlays directly or indirectly related to the Manpower Economy Project would involve a disproportionate amount of work, but some typical examples are given below:

(a) *Redeployment of Training Tasks.* With the aim of concentrating training more cost-effectively, it was decided to transfer the training tasks at RAF Manby and RAF Spitalgate to other locations enabling these two stations to be closed. This involved capital works expenditure of £62,000 at Leeming and Cranwell, which absorbed the Manby tasks, but there was a saving of 52 Service and 184 civilian posts, costed at £0·5 million per annum, as well as savings in station running costs (works maintenance, fuel and light, etc.) at Manby. The closure of Spitalgate is not yet completed but will involve works costs of about £100,000 at Hereford and Newton. It will save about 80 Service and 56 civilian posts (costing £0·3 million per annum) as well as the Spitalgate running costs.

(b) *Recording of Aircraft Incidents.* It is an Air Traffic Control requirement to record all RT communications for the purpose of investigating aircraft incidents and near miss reports. By installing tape recording facilities at certain Strike Command stations (capital cost of £21,000) it was possible to save 9 airmen posts with a saving of £15,000 per annum.

Major Individual Economies

4. The Manpower Economy Project comprises two phases. Phase I, which was completed in 1972, consisted of an all-out campaign throughout the Royal Air Force to identify posts which could be disestablished with acceptable risks, without changing basic policies and without damaging the operational effectiveness of the RAF. It was therefore essentially a severe belt-tightening process comprising reductions in most establishments in the RAF.

5. Phase II is a deeper exercise seeking economies in manpower mainly through reviewing policies, tasks (both the need for them and the method of performing them), organisation, deployments and procedures in order to reduce manpower and support costs to the minimum. This phase of the exercise involves a very large number of individual projects many of them small but significant in total. Some examples of the larger savings, in addition to those already mentioned in paragraph 3, are given below:

    (a) *Revised Policy for Ground Radio Servicing Flights.* A study of ground radio servicing procedures disclosed that it was practicable to utilise the spare time of night watchkeepers on servicing work. This results in a substantial saving in day staffs and produces recurrent savings of 150 Service posts costing £0·4 million per annum.

    (b) *Revised Apprentice Entry Schemes.* With the advent of the higher school leaving age in 1972, which would then have necessitated changes in any case, it was decided that the apprentice entry schemes should be drastically reduced with increased recruitment of adults in view of the economic advantages. An adult fitter with a Mathematics and Science GCE can, for example, be fully trained in about one year instead of the two years for Craft apprentices of a lower educational standard. There have therefore been substantial savings in training staff. (Recurrent manpower savings: 210 Service posts costed at £0·6 million per annum.)

    (c) *Nimrod Aircraft—Aircrew Requirements.* Following investigations by Strike Command, it was decided that peace-time operations for Nimrod aircraft could be satisfactorily achieved with a reduction in the total number of aircrew established for the squadrons. This has resulted in manpower savings of 48 Service posts costing £0·2 million per annum.

Improved Efficiency and Co-ordination

6. The examples quoted above are generally expected, as are most of the individual projects within Phase II of the Economy exercise, to lead to improved efficiency and co-ordination. The redeployment of training tasks on fewer stations has been accompanied by a streamlining of the Training Command controlling structure with the elimination of one Group Headquarters thus enabling the Command Headquarters to exercise better co-ordination and control of ground training without involving an intermediate organisation.

7. Other examples include the rationalisation of all Mobile Air Movements Sections in the UK by combining them into one unit at RAF Lyneham which has saved 50 Service posts; the transfer of responsibility for checking on standards achieved by trainees from the " user " Commands to Training Command, with recurrent savings of 29 Service posts; and the transfer of certain radar training for navigators from the Strike Command Bombing School to a Vulcan Operational Conversion Unit, enabling three aircraft to be disestablished and 50 Service posts to be saved.

Reductions in Service and Civilian Numbers

8. As already mentioned, the posts saved to date comprise 5,872 Service and 1,471 civilian posts. Consequential reductions in the numbers of Service personnel borne have been achieved by normal wastage, relaxation of restrictions on voluntary retirements, and adjustments in recruiting and re-engagement levels but in addition a limited redundancy programme involving about 500 officers and 900 airmen has been carried out. The compensation payments for redundancy amount to £3·7 million. On the civilian side, the rundown has been achieved almost entirely through normal wastage and restriction of recruitment where necessary.

August, 1974.

RAF ORGANISATION REVIEW (D.33)

Memorandum by the Ministry of Defence (SCOE 69/1)

1. We understand that the Committee wish to have further information about the results of the review of the RAF support organisation and of the organisation within the Ministry of Defence for engineering and supply support of the RAF.

Organisation within the MOD for Engineering and Supply Support of the RAF

2. The review indicated that the close relationship between engineering and supply functions would benefit from a greater degree of integration at all levels. Accordingly, the staffs of the Directorate General of Engineering and the Directorate General of Supply were integrated in November 1973 to form a Controllerate of Engineering and Supply. The new organisation which is still in process of settling down is expected to result in improved efficiency. Economies in staffs are also expected but it is too early to make a reliable estimate of the numbers. So far the number of Directorates has reduced from twelve to ten and further streamlining is in progress.

The RAF Support Organisation

3. The role of Maintenance Command was the management of the storage, repair and issue of equipment, including complete aircraft to the RAF. No. 90 Group, an independent formation, provided repair and servicing support for ground radars, airfield and navigation aids and telecommunications. The review suggested the need to concentrate at a single Headquarters responsibility for support activities. Support Command was formed on 1st September, 1973 to take over the functions of Maintenance Command and No. 90 Group and to exercise administrative control of RAF hospitals and certain other medical establishments in the UK. It is expected that the merger will enable economies to be made by rationalising the activities of certain units with broadly similar engineering tasks. This will take some time to work out. In the meantime some staff economies as a result of the merger of Headquarters staffs have been made and more are expected. Support Command Headquarters is at Andover in accommodation formerly occupied by Headquarters Maintenance Command.

December 1974.

SERVICE MANPOWER ECONOMY (D.34)

Memorandum by the Ministry of Defence (SCOE 69/2)

The Sub-Committee asked for further information in the form of answers to four questions listed in the Clerk's letter of 26th November. The questions and the Ministry's answers are below:

1. *In what significant ways and to what extent was the Centre involved in the RAF Manpower Economy project?*

The inception of the RAF Manpower Review was known at a high level throughout the Ministry of Defence. The Review was however initiated and prosecuted by the Air Force Department and the Central Staffs were not significantly involved.

2. *Before the project started, was consideration given to the possibility of mounting an all-Service manpower economy drive?*

The drive for manpower economy is continuous in all three Services. Each uses the methods and machinery most suited to their purposes. In view of the separate studies and reorganisations in progress in the Navy and Army Departments, referred to below, it was not considered appropriate to widen the RAF Manpower Review to cover all three Services.

3. *Has a comparable project been undertaken since 1971 by either the Army or the Navy?   If so, when did it start and what net savings are expected as a result?*

Royal Navy

Over the past decade, the Royal Navy has not infrequently been unable to meet its recruiting targets and has therefore been obliged to keep manpower levels under constant scrutiny.   As it happens, in recent years manpower shortages, especially in technical grades, have given rise to increasing concern, and because of this a system of manpower allocation was introduced in 1972. This relates annually the total requirement for Naval manpower to the forecast availability, and tasks of lowest priority are then given up.   It is intended as a permanent method of manpower control and it is expected that about 500 Naval posts ashore will be reduced by April 1975.

More generally, a Sub-Committee of the Admiralty Board (known as the Way Ahead Committee) was reconstituted in 1967 in the wake of the previous Defence Review, with the object of mounting studies into particular areas of Naval activity such as the shore support organisations and the Naval Command structure.   Many of these studies aimed at, and succeeded in, achieving manpower savings.

Army

The economical use of manpower is a key factor in the Army's programme and plans because it is a manpower intensive organisation in which emphasis is on the deployment of well-equipped men in the field force rather than on the manning of sophisticated weapons systems.   The main instrument of control is the stringent allocation of UK trained officers and soldiers to approved tasks closely screened by the Army's machinery for manpower accounting and establishment inspection and review.   The need for strict priorities to maximise fighting strength is reinforced by recruiting shortfalls which often effectively limit the manpower available.   Control over civilian numbers and the balance between military and civilian manpower is no less strict.

A special Manpower Review to supplement existing arrangements for Manpower control was not considered necessary in 1971 because a number of reorganisations were already in progress the main ones being:

(*a*) The reorganisation (including use of ADP) of the Army's Manning and Record Offices ; this has saved 560 out of 2,193 civilian posts since 1967 ;

(*b*) The reorganisation of the UK Land Forces Command Structure completed in 1973 ;

(*c*) The introduction of the RAOC's computer based Central Inventory Control Point for controlling the Army's supply and provisioning system worldwide ;

(*d*) Reorganisation of Junior Training, begun in 1969, and completed in 1973, led to a saving of about 250 Service and 350 civilian posts.

4. *If no such comparable project has been undertaken is one now being planned and when is it expected to start?*

All future plans are overshadowed by the Defence Review. In the Navy a number of studies are currently in progress aimed at providing savings in manpower both service and civilians. In the Army the object will be to achieve the considerable reductions required to the greatest extent possible by structural adjustment; by examining the span of command, the size and number of headquarters, the concentration of specialised functions etc with the object of maintaining the maximum combat capability and fire power.

6th December 1974.

Examination of Witnesses

Mr. A. D. HARVEY, Assistant Under-Secretary of State (Organisation) (Air), Mr. F. C. HERD, Assistant Under-Secretary of State (Personnel) (Defence Secretariat), Mr. J. D. BRYARS, Assistant Under-Secretary of State (General Staff), Rear Admiral R. D. LYGO, Director-General of Naval Manpower and Training, Mr. P. V. COTTER, Head of R.A.F. Organisation and Establishments Finance Division, and Air Commodore B. W. PARSONS, Director of Establishments and Management Services (R.A.F.), Ministry of Defence, called in and examined.

Chairman.

111. Good afternoon, Gentlemen. We have read this statement about what the RAF did and we were very impressed with the way they cut down their manpower. We hope they did this without cutting down their efficiency. We thought we would like to ask them certain questions. We did ask for a senior witness from the Centre of the Ministry to come today and we are grateful to see Mr. Herd again. First, what we would like to do is to ask some general questions of the RAF. Then we should like to hear a little from the Centre and then finally put a few questions to the Royal Navy and the Army. We are impressed by the RAF initiative by starting a real saving campaign in manpower, and it proved to be savings to the extent of about £20 million a year. It is very refreshing after the arbitrary defence cuts we examined earlier this year. Could you please start by describing to the Committee fairly briefly how this project came to be set up and how it was managed? How big was the project team and how did it operate?——(*Mr. Harvey*.) I think it originated in the gradual and growing realisation in the Air Force Department that the proportion of the budget which was going on manpower was gradually rising. The Air Force Board were aware of this and clearly if the trend continued there was going to be less and less money available, or a smaller proportion available for equipment and for the front line generally. So in early 1971 we tried a pilot experiment in Strike Command of which Sir Andrew Humphrey was then Commander in Chief, and that produced extremely encouraging results, and so it was applied to the Air Force as a whole throughout the world. I would not want to suggest that all the economies that took place were as a direct result of that project because a number of them I think certainly would have taken place anyway. I think it gave a great impetus and what was important was that the motivation was there. It became widely known in the Air Force that this really was the only way of reversing the trend and trying to strengthen the front line. As the paper explained, it was divided into two parts. The first phase was just belt tightening, which is the sort of thing you can only do once. You cannot go on doing it. Having tightened your belt and it is up to the last notch, after a period you can do it again, but basically it is a once and for all thing. The second phase was to look round for all sorts of ways of reducing the cost of operating and supporting the Royal Air Force. We did put a few examples in the paper. There were a great many suggestions of this sort, some of them quite small. I do not want to suggest all this was something completely unusual. It was

something that goes on all the time. It goes on in the Navy and Army as well as the Air Force, but it was given a bit of impetus by reasons underlying it, and, frankly, by Sir Andrew Humphrey's personality in Strike Command in starting it off.

112. It was an Air Board decision and I am not surprised to hear Air Marshal Humphrey's name mentioned in this connection. What pressures were put on the branches under scrutiny? Did all branches enter into the spirit of the operation?——I think Air Commodore Parsons could answer this. He was in Strike Command at the time. After the initial phase it had to be sold to people and presentations were given explaining the reasons. I think it caught on and I think Air Commodore Parsons would agree that people did get the spirit of the thing and it went ahead without any great pressure. (Air Commodore *Parsons*). I think that is quite a fair comment. The main drive was really down the executive net. I was in fact Sir Andrew Humphrey's appointed officer for running the project at the time before I took up my present appointment. I reported directly to him on all matters concerning this exercise. The thing was played so you went from your commander in chief, to your group commanders, to your station commanders, and they were all invited to make suggestions. This crossed the Branch boundaries of professions because they were all brought in at different levels to make their contributions and advise what they thought could be done to meet the economy target set for them.

113. How big was your team for this job?——I had two other officers. There were the three of us for the purpose of monitoring it because we were using the normal staff chain. There was no need for a large team. I think it is important you should operate it through the normal staff network because the key thing is to get the motivation right. You cannot tell people about economy and get the last drops out of the system.

114. Would you say to one station, "Another station has made this economy, would you do the same"?—— Not particularly, no. My job would have been to say, for example, "It is possible to do certain things, maybe technical or traffic control, on another station, what do you think about that?" My function was cross-fertilisation. They had the targets from the Commander in Chief. My job was to say, "What do you think of it?" The commander could get his target by whatever means he liked. He was left with what he decided to do.

115. When you say "their targets", did you fix a target percentage?——In general terms, yes.

Mr. *Finsberg*.

116. Mr. Harvey said that one would not regard this as something special and that it goes on all the time. Could he give us two examples of other projects of this nature?——(Mr. *Harvey*.) I was not thinking in terms of general projects, but in terms of redeployment leading to closures of stations and economies of that sort; the sort of thing one is looking for all the time.

117. Could you give us a couple of examples, and give us an idea of what the savings were?——Not directly connected with the Defence Review?

118. In the context of what you said in your answer?——I think one example would be in Training Command where because of the run down in the Far East from the last Defence Review, and because to some extent of the other reductions we were making, there was obviously a reduction in one's intake, and therefore in the training requirement. It was clear that unless this was picked up there would be some under-utilisation of training resources. Part of the exercise, and this was not particularly part of the economy review as such, was to work out a new redeployment of one's training resources to move certain training tasks from one place to another where there was spare capacity, and that in fact took place and has been announced.

Mr. *Boyden*.

119. I am very interested in what the Air Commodore said about getting the people to come along to agree on this. I was very active in the changes that took place when the Ministry of Public

Buildings and Works was created. I wonder if any of you have the experience of what happened in 1963-64 on this. I was told the only way to do it was to impose it, and in fact the permanent secretary of the Ministry of Works, or whatever he was called, did not know about it until it had happened. You were all concerned because your works departments were drawn from you and put in the centre. Can any of you comment on that from your experience of those years? This is 1963-64. It is the exact opposite of the Air Commodore's theory?——I was not directly concerned with that, but I can confirm what you say. It was not known by people below the top level until the last moment. This was a major organisational change on which there were bound to be different views. What we are talking about here is a manpower review with general economies as the object, stemming from an underlying cause which everybody could understand. I think that is something quite different. If we tried radically to alter the organisation of the Air Force that would be another matter to put across.

120. It is a rather important point where the line comes. If it is within an organisation where the boundaries are clear, and you know what it is, you can do it. There might be a strong argument that this is the best way to do it?——You can say, with the achievement you are aiming at, that unless there are manpower economies there is going to be great difficulty in finding enough money for equipment and for the front line in the Air Force generally and we want everybody to co-operate in thinking up ways in which support costs can be cut. That is the sort of thing everybody can subscribe to.

121. Perhaps the Air Commodore might like to come in on this?——(Air Commodore *Parsons*.) I think there is a difference in the example you quote because what we were trying to do was to get the whole of a very sophisticated and complex organisation to look at everything it does and see whether or not we could do it in a most cost effective way. We have between a million and a quarter and a million and a half items on our inventory. We operate 36 types of aircraft. It is very difficult from the outside to analyse a thing like that and impose something on it and to be sure that your system of checks and balances still prevents you taking risks. We wanted our professionals to say, " I think I can accept a slightly different standard of service for a particular part of an engine ", and to be happy with any risks involved. I have an example in mind at the moment, where we saved quite a bit of money, but if it had gone wrong (and we lost a vital aeroplane) the whole thing would have been different. You have got to bring them all in with you. We were after everyone's ideas. We really went down to the corporals and the airmen and said, " We have this problem about manpower and cost in relation to support on the front line, what do you think about it? " We got literally hundreds of suggestions. A lot of them did not amount to much, but that did not matter because psychologically you wanted to get everyone involved. That is what was different from just an organisational change.

122. I do not think it was so very different. I am really delighted with what you say. I always advocated doing it in the way the Air Force has done it   Rationalising building is not as complicated as the Air Force. Building is a complicated business, but it is not as complicated as dealing with the Air Force. I should think yours was more difficult. I was quite fascinated by the achievement. We have read about the achievement, that it was done in this way of consultations. It is very good.

Mr. *Kershaw*.

123. The indication you have given, that everybody was asked to think up some sort of way in which economies for manpower could be made, is obviously a very good idea from the point of view of morale and getting the enthusiasm of everybody concerned. It nevertheless seems to me a little erratic and planless. I am sure it was not and I would like you to indicate what were the lines of inquiry which in the end proved most fruitful? Was it the case, for example, that the abolition of a senior post resulted in the reduction of junior posts which were, so to speak, servicing that senior post? ——We did put that kind of situation

but it is a bit difficult really to answer it in that form, because as everyone was being asked to think how they might put forward ideas to help—I stress this because I wanted to get the picture across that we did go right down to the airman and that level—the main drive was directed at the staffs and the executives. The station commander knew that his group commander wanted a certain percentage of savings and any other suggestions which he could make as a practising operator to somehow or other try to get us more sharp end and less back end. We did not get the same sort of offers from different people. Different stations have different tasks. Even two fighter stations in different locations have slightly different tasks, so you do not get the same answers from them. I cannot say just how I could relate it ; I find it rather difficult. I do not know how to meet your requirement.

124. You mentioned there are a million and a quarter to a million and a half items on the inventory. To what extent did the introduction of computers result in the saving of manpower in looking after that?——The computer is handling our inventory now and we hope to improve the method of inventory handling by computer. The answer is that it had been done before this ; it had been planned before this project started and the method of bringing it onto the computer is going on all the time. There are still methods by which we think we can improve the processing.

125. Did the computer reduce or increase the number of people employed?——It reduced the number of people employed.

126. To what extent did reclassification of trades have any effect?——I do not think we reclassified any trades in this particular exercise

127. Do you think reclassification would reduce a number of people?—— There was one that we put together. I do not know the answer to that because this really falls into a continuing process which is still going on largely on the training side, which we have not finished with by any means.

128. The RAF has comparatively few front line personnel because of the com-

paratively few people who fly aeroplanes compared to the main force. To what extent do you think the methods employed therefore would be useful to the other services which have more front line personnal?——I think the philosophy is all right. The thought behind it is fine, but each service will have a different problem. I would not wish to argue and say one thing is particularly suitable for them or not. I honestly do not know, except it is always good to take that approach to the problem.

129. There is one arm of the RAF which is different, the RAF Regiment. Can you point to any savings of personnel?——Not at that time. We are reviewing it now.

Chairman.

130. We will move to Note 2, general results of the project. You show in your paper that over 7,000 posts have already been saved. You also say that Phase I ended in 1972, and we infer that Phase II is still in progress. Could you please say how many of the posts already saved, split between Service and Civilian are attributable to Phase I and how many to Phase II ; and how many more posts do you expect to have saved by the end of Phase II? Leave quite apart the reductions which were announced the other day?——(Mr. *Harvey*.) I do not think we could split the savings resulting from Phase I from those in Phase II. We have give in the first paper the total for both. That was 5,872 Service posts and 1,471 Civilian posts. I think when one comes to consider the continuing effect of Phase II we run into the current Defence Review and I think some of the savings we might have made will be subsumed within that. I think it becomes rather blurred. It is impossible to say savings will be made in the future which were due to this or that or would have occurred anyway.

131. Do you reckon the project is at an end now?——I think if there had not been a Defence Review it would have gone on, with diminishing returns. You would have got something out of it. We have got to have a review of a different sort which is how you get the background and support savings.

132. You have made no estmiate of what you might have saved by what

10 *December*, 1974.]   Mr. A. D. HARVEY, Mr. F. C. HERD,   [*Continued.*
Mr. J. D. BRYARS, Rear Admiral R. D. LYGO, Mr. P. V. COTTER
and Air Commodore B. W. PARSONS.

would have been the end of Phase II? It is sort of a continuing thing?——It is a little hypothetical. Had there been no Defence Review what other savings would we have made? I would rather not chance a guess on that.

Dr. *Miller.*

133. In the saving of something like 7,000 posts, how do you manage to achieve a situation of only 1,400 people being made redundant? Is this due to not taking up in recruitment? Is it a recruitment situation?——It took place over a period which means you can reduce intake ; you can rely on wastage ; you can be easier in allowing applications for voluntary retirement and that sort of thing. One tried to use other methods to reduce redundancy to the minimum, not only because it is bad management but it is also expensive.

134. For 500 and 900, making 1,400, you save something like over 7,000 posts. Over what sort of period of time is that?——That is over a period of three years.

Chairman.

135. We will pass on to what we term Note 3. These are really specific savings. You have given several examples of large individual savings in Phase II. We were especially interested to see that you have been able to make impressive savings, such as the new arrangements for ground radio servicing, virtually by administrative action, and without incurring capital expenditure. I do not say this in any hostile spirit, but the examples you have given are typical and you could produce other examples? You have not picked particularly the top ones for the paper you have given us?——No, I think we tried to pick fairly typical examples. We tried to produce striking examples that would illustrate the point. I do not think we have been selective. I think you can always say of any example that it looks a good idea, but why did you not do it earlier. Perhaps that is the answer in the one you quoted. It is a thing that could have been done at any time that people got around to thinking about it.

Mr. *Boyden.*

136. Could I take a specific example? The Nimrod. You have reduced the size of the crew?——(Air Commodore *Parsons.*) Not the size of the crew but the ratio of crews to the aircraft.

137. Could you explain why you could do that in peace time when presumably you would go back on it in war time?——No. It was adjusted for a war time rate. With an aircraft of that type we have to keep it at the war time rate : we could not provide that kind of sophisticated crew without continuous training so they must be there, and at the ratio we would use in war time.

138. How was this able to be done?——As we started off with a new aircraft, we first had to make judgments as to what we needed to get an effective ratio over a long period of time. When we gained experience and when the C.-in-C. asked " Is your strength at present really necessary? " we got them (Operators) thinking hard and they came up with a slightly lower ratio of crews to aircraft. We then had to test it. It is the checks and balances which are essential. We had to wait until we had mounted flying exercises, bringing crews into the NATO exercises and putting them under pressure simulating a war time condition to see if they were happy.

139. You are not putting them under a strain on the Nimrod. You are satisfied?——That was the point, and why we had to watch it. You have to go back to your professionals all the time, whoever they may be, because if you do not you can impose something which is unrealistic.

Chairman.

140. Perhaps we might turn to Note 4. There are now two further important points I wish to clear with the RAF before we go on to the other witnesses. The first point is this : can we be assured that the manpower economy project has not resulted in any marked loss of efficiency? Are the RAF absolutely confident that these savings will not weaken the front line to any significant extent?——Absolutely certain.

10 *December*, 1974.]   Mr. A. D. HARVEY, Mr. F. C. HERD,   [*Continued.*
Mr. J. D. BRYARS, Rear Admiral R. D. LYGO, Mr. P. V. COTTER
and Air Commodore B. W. PARSONS.

141. You are absolutely positive?——
Yes.

Dr. *Miller.*

142. Can I go back to the Nimrod for a moment? It does say that this refers to peace time operations for Nimrod and not wartime?——(Mr. *Harvey*.) I think the point Air Commodore Parsons was making was that with an aircraft like the Nimrod the peace time operations are the same as the war time operations.

Sir *F. Bennett.*

143. This Note 4 reflects an earlier misgiving of mine. Is it felt that having made on their own initiative some extraordinarily striking and helpful reductions that they have now been dealt a second blow by the additional cuts? In other words, if they had not made them at all, would they now be in a better position? Is it felt by those who give a lead that it is rather a pity they made the gesture in the first place? I wonder if they felt these cuts would not have been in this form if they had not been given the initiative in the first place. It would be unfortunate if every time they make a gesture they feel they suffer further reductions because they have shown they can make reductions?——We feel that the reductions we made before this started were all valuable contributions to the total reductions we have got to make ultimately because the constrictions are in terms of the percentage of the GNP to be spent on defence and in terms of a total allocation for the Air Force which would have been the same whether we started to make reductions or not. I think we felt we would be off to a good start for the other reductions we now have to make which will be accompanied by reductions in tasks and commitments as well.

144. It is not an easy thing to put it accurately. Supposing you had not made 5,000 already, would you still have been 18,000 or do you think you would have had to be 23,000?——I was saying earlier that not all these economies can be attributed to the economy review. Some of them would have happened anyway or should have happened anyway. To the extent that we may have speeded them up a bit and increased the progress towards economy, I think those reductions would have had to have been

made anyway as part of our present Defence Review if we had not made them before.

Dr. *Miller.*

145. In connection with these reductions were you surprised at all at the extent of the Air Force reductions compared with the other two services, or was this a concerted effort? Were you surprised? Have you any comments on that? It does seem a rather heavy burden, that the brunt of the reductions apparently was borne by the RAF. Were you surprised when it came out this way? ——I am not sure I ought to comment on that. I do not mean from a security point of view, but I think the attribution of the Defence Review reductions between the services is a matter which you settle when you settle what commitments and tasks are going to be given up. It is inherent in the broad policy decision.

146. You did this completely on your own?——The Air Force manpower review which we have been talking about up to now, do you mean?

147. You did that completely on your own?——Yes, for internal reasons we were unhappy about the proportions of the budget spent on manpower.

Mr. *Boyden.*

148. Presumably when you were looking at manpower you were not in a position to say you could get rid of this type of aircraft, for example, because this is really at a higher level, but I suppose there must be decisions like that. We saw it, for example, with ships. We were on a ship in the Mediterranean and the captain convinced us quickly that if they had a new ship they would save a lot of bodies. Where does that argument come into manpower savings?——To take a minor example, we did get rid of an aircraft; that was the Bassett. It was not inherently a part of this exercise.

149. The staff on an RAF station would not be in a position to say, "Let's get rid of this aircraft"?——There would be nothing to stop them giving a proposal, and it would be looked at.

10 *December*, 1974.]   Mr. A. D. HARVEY, Mr. F. C. HERD,   [*Continued.*
Mr. J. D. BRYARS, Rear Admiral R. D. LYGO, Mr. P. V. COTTER
and Air Commodore B. W. PARSONS.

150. Did anything like this happen? ——(Air Commodore *Parsons*.) It was not practicable because we had a policy restraint from the Government to do certain things, and if you have that constraint you cannot get rid of the equipment to do it.

Mr. *Kershaw.*

151. with regard to Training Command, it seems to me there must be a temptation to reduce Training Command in peace time to what you need basically to fly the aeroplanes without taking into consideration casualties. Are you satisfied that the reductions have taken into account the war time casualties?——I think they are related to the basic problem which is the aircraft. The fundamental thing is, how many aircraft have you got? What is your estimate of your battle casualties? The next step is, how many pilots have I got and how many can I drop? If you consider the exercise like that at the moment we are happy.

152. What about servicing the aircraft——We do use the ground men from Training Command when the training stops in an emergency.

153. The RAF, as I understand it, has embarked on a rather larger programme of doing its own servicing than at one time they thought necessary, and frankly because they had been getting such a poor service out of their civilian people. Now that civilian people seem to have more time on their own hands is there more prospect of the RAF going back to them?——(Mr. *Harvey*.) I can only think of one example and that was because of a particular contractor who had difficulty in recruiting tradesmen.

154. Rolls-Royce made a proper mess, did they not? Have you considered going slow on St. Athan and giving it back to civilian contractors?——We are setting up a new line at St. Athan to service the Adour engine.

155. Is that increase of manpower at St. Athan?——It is matched by other things that are moving out. It leaves the manpower about the same.

156. It is increase of manpower in the RAF as a whole which results from taking work away from civilian contractors?——In the case of Jaguar it was not with civilian contractors.

157. Have you increased the amount the RAF are doing or have you not? ——In that particular case, yes.

Chairman.

158. Would I be right in thinking the whole of the 18,000 reduction and consequent civilian reductions will follow from reductions in specific tasks? If you do not want to answer it, leave it. Do you have to cut a specific task to get these reductions?——Yes.

159. Would you agree that this very worthwhile project that you carried out was started at the top by the Air Board and was carried out by a small team which engaged the whole spirit of the Air Force to bring these reductions about? Did you see the £20 million spent on hardware?——We saw an improvement certainly in the front line resulting from it.

160. You cannot say, but there was an improvement?——(Air Commodore *Parsons*.) We did not really have the time. We have now got involved in our second Defence Review.

161. Now we will turn to Mr. Herd. Having listened to the RAF witnesses, and I know you knew all this before, you would agree this has been a rewarding project. We found your paper answering our four specific questions a little disappointing. First, we were disappointed to see that the Central Staffs played little part in the RAF project. That was so, was it not? It was very much an RAF project?——(Mr. *Herd*.) Yes, it was. To some extent it would have been counter productive if we had intervened. I think you have heard Air Commodore Parsons explain how the motivation was effective because it came from within the RAF. I think to some extent if there had been any imposition of outside inspectors the motivation might not have worked so well.

162. Secondly, while the answers to questions 3 and 4 quote some useful manpower savings, they do not suggest that the other Services' efforts have been anywhere near as detailed or as exten-

sive as the RAF's project. There may be reasons for this?——Can I say a few words about the position of the other two services in general about the time the RAF exercise was starting. There were some significant differences. In the first place, I do not think they were quite so concerned as the RAF were about the proportion of their costs that were going on teeth and tail equipment and manpower. I do not think they were quite so concerned with the rises in their manpower costs. For one thing, the other two services were in a very much more difficult recruiting situation. For some reason the Army and the Navy throughout that period were finding it far more difficult to get recruits than the RAF were and that was to some extent imposing an automatic restraint on manpower which we did not welcome particularly, but it did enforce very stringent standards of manning throughout the Army and Navy. I would not like to give the impression they were doing nothing to economise on manpower. They were doing a great deal and this recruiting shortage was forcing them to do that.

Mr. *Boyden.*

163. Could you give an example of that? I am thinking of the command structure?——I cannot out of my head give an example, but my colleagues may be able to think of one.

164. How many jobs did the general review of the command structure save? ——(Mr. *Bryars.*) I cannot remember offhand—I think of the order of 150 military posts and 900 civilian.

165. Were there other things going on?——(Mr. *Herd.*) Yes, we have listed some in the paper. It is a continuous process, the scrutiny of manpower in the other two services.

Mr. *Kershaw.*

166. Can I ask if you are able to give any examples of the reduction of the number of people employed in the MOD matching the reductions in the troops in the field?——The numbers have dropped off over the years, but it is true that they have not probably dropped proportionately. One of the things is that the bur-

den of successive Defence Reviews has fallen on the Ministry of Defence itself. It has been difficult to cut numbers in the Ministry in the face of the reorganisation and the Defence Reviews that have been going on over the last few years. One of the essential factors for a reduction in numbers at headquarters is a period of stability, but I do take the point that we ought to bend our efforts towards increasing reductions of the Ministry of Defence staff and we are always under continual pressure to do that.

167. What about the commands that have been merged? Has that resulted in reductions?——Yes, that has resulted in considerable reductions. The Navy are now down to one sea command and one land command. The Army came down to a single land command and those measures did result in considerable reductions.

Mr. *Boyden.*

168. Have ther been economies in stores administration? Has that been developing?——Yes, I think there have been fairly consant reductions. To some extent I think the stores reductions have been linked in with computerisation as was mentioned earlier, but the two things march hand in hand.

169. Is there anything right across the three services on this? Can the Army learn from the Air Force and can the Air Force learn from the Army?—— There are certainly examples of concentration of computer processes and how computers can help with the handling of stores and such things. There are common committees on which problems connected with inventory control and computer control are discussed.

170. The Army made a good deal of saving on pay. Was this picked up by the other services?——Yes, I think it was. Actually I think the pay process went on in parallel. I think the services were all mechanising their pay or computerising their pay at roughly the same period of time and they learnt from one another. (Mr. *Harvey.*) There is a central computer division which advises. On the whole that would ensure the sort of thing you mention.

10 *December*, 1974.]   Mr. A. D. HARVEY, Mr. F. C. HERD,   [*Continued.*
Mr. J. D. BRYARS, Rear Admiral R. D. LYGO, Mr. P. V. COTTER
and Air Commodore B. W. PARSONS.

Mr. *Sandelson.*

171. I would like to enquire about the revised apprentice entry schemes. Is there any difficulty in recruiting adult fitters with higher educational standards on entry to replace the younger apprentices in the earlier scheme?——(Mr. *Herd.*) Are you speaking across the board?

172. I am speaking about the Air Force?——(Air Commodore *Parsons.*) There are no problems so far.

173. Do you advertise in the ordinary way for fitters of this kind?——I know recruiting publicity goes on, but I have not noticed it. That is not my side.

174. Does it involve a change in the number of people engaged in this work as between the younger ones and the adult fitters, and at what age does an adult apprentice commence?——(Mr. *Harvey.*) I do not think any of us are familiar with this.

Mr. *Sandelson.*] These are rather esoteric points. I think it is important to maintain the standard of people in this field and their availability for the services.

Chairman.

175. If there are no more questions for Mr. Herd perhaps I could put one. Do you think looking back that possibly from the Centre—and the Committee might take this sort of view—it would really be reasonable if you suggest similar projects be carried out by the Royal Navy and the Army? They might turn up some surprising and dramatic savings. You have never thought there ought to be more pressure?——(Mr. *Herd.*) It is a difficult question. I would not say it was an unreasonable view to take at all. Whether it would prove as useful is a matter for speculation. It might well have done so, but we might have found that the degree of saving available because of the different circumstances would have been of a very much smaller order. I would not like to speculate. The position we all find ourselves in now is that the Defence Review is imposing altogether new parameters across the field, and indeed the Defence Review was talked about, thought about

and was beginning to get under way in the early part of this year.

176. Yes, because of the cuts made by the previous government?——The cuts made by the previous government is not what I was thinking of so much as the institution of the Defence Review in the spring of this year.

177. Did you ever think at the Centre about asking the Royal Navy and the Army to do something similar and turn it down perhaps, or not?——No. I would not like to give the impression that we were working in watertight compartments in the Ministry of Defence. Everything that is being done in one part of the Ministry of Defence is well known throughout the Ministry. It was well known I think to the Army and the Navy that the manpower economy exercise was going on. Whether we should have pressed them harder to do something along those lines is a difficult question to answer. The fact is that the role of the Centre, as we conceive it at the moment, is to allocate resources, to play a leading role in the general allocation of resources, but the management is left to the service boards. The management of service manpower is so intimately connected with the detailed organisation of the services, as you hear from the examples given by the Air Ministry, that I think it is part of the responsibility of management to see that service manpower is used economically. I am a little sceptical about whether the intervention of an outsider who will be regarded as " them " would have been effective in securing the maximum economy. (Mr. *Harvey.*) Perhaps I could just say that I think the same sort of idea would have to take a different form, in the other two services in any case. Our attack on manpower was a way of trying to transfer resources from the tail, the support area, to the teeth. For the Army that would take quite a different form and perhaps it would be for the Navy. It seems that the Navy's Way Ahead Committee mentioned in the last paper is very much the same idea as the RAF point of view. I think the same idea would be interpreted in different ways. It is the general theme of transferring money from the support area to the teeth.

10 *December*, 1974.]   Mr. A. D. HARVEY, Mr. F. C. HERD,   [*Continued.*
Mr. J. D. BRYARS, Rear Admiral R. D. LYGO, Mr. P. V. COTTER
and Air Commodore B. W. PARSONS.

178. Could I now put a question or two to the Royal Navy and Army witnesses. We know there have been recruiting difficulties during recent years which have caused some pressure on manpower. There have also been times when the recruiting has been quite good, in 1971, for example. We also recognise that valuable savings have been made as shown in the answers to our questions 3 and 4[1], but these do not seem to reflect a concerted drive for manpower savings comparable to the RAF's work. I just wonder whether you think something like this could possibly have been done or could have been followed, though I realise the general Defence Review is cutting across the future?——(Rear Admiral *Lygo*.) As my Air Force colleagues have made a point of saying, I think it is important not to get this whole matter out of perspective. In fact, in the same period within the Royal Navy we reduced our command structure quite drastically from three home commanders in chief to one[2]. We abolished all overseas commands of any size and we reduced to one Commander-in-Chief Fleet. That is a reduction in command structure which is much more severe than has been achieved by the other two services. As a result of the committee's recommendation we are in the process of reducing 20 shore establishments. We have in the last two years reduced manpower, civilian and service, by 8,000, and I think when you dwell on those figures you will realise that we have not exactly been slothful in pursuing manpower economies because we recognise in a very clear fashion in the Navy that everything ashore effectively is something we do not want and we must concentrate all our efforts into ships which hopefully float. The division of support and teeth to us is very clear and we are always focussing on this. It is true that we have approached these savings from different standpoints. We have been forecasting for the last four years a steady deficit in next year's account of manpower, and this has always meant we have had to ration manpower to the non-essential area, and that has meant transferring men from shore to sea. The figures I have given you are some indication of the measure of success we have achieved.

179. Was the cut forced on you by recruiting, or have you saved jobs without cutting the efficiency of the service?——The situation we faced was a steady deficit in the year ahead so we were forced to make the same economies that the Air Force has made in anticipation of the fact that we just would not have the men, which was a much more rigorous discipline.

180. Do you think you have lost any efficiency?——That is very difficult to quantify. The fleet remains at the same size as it was when we started.

Mr. *Sandelson*.

181. With regard to the efficiency point which is of paramount importance, clearly it is all very well maintaining the strength of the Navy in terms of the number of ships, but if manpower shortages deliberately brought about are going to reduce efficiency that is something we would wish to avoid and examine carefully?——I do not think there is any evidence. We have had our mind sharpened by these deficiencies in manpower; we have made savings which probably we would not have made if this situation had not been presenting itself. The discipline which motivated the Air Force was the percentage of their total budget which was dedicated to manpower; ours also was rising at about the same time as theirs was but it has fallen—8 per cent of the total Naval budget over the same period. This discipline was also necessary to us but the savings have been produced in a different way for a different reason. At the moment there has been no reduction in efficiency.

Mr. *Kershaw*.

182. The result has been that the men spend more time at sea?——In general this is true. The pattern of fleet operations has also changed in that time to the extent that we no longer deploy ships for as long a period away as one time we used to. This resulted from the political decisions to withdraw gradually from our overseas commitments so it has accidentally timed itself correctly with what we were doing.

---

[1] See pages 42-43.
[2] *Note by Witness:* This was done under the auspices of the Way Ahead Committee

Chairman.

183. Could I turn to the Army? You heard the question I put to the Navy. Would you like to comment on that? ——(Mr. *Bryars*.) On the question of special manpower saving economies?

184. Do you feel something more could have been done or are the circumstances in the Army so different?—— The circumstances in the Army differ to some extent because the front line in the Army is formed more by the armed man than by the manned weapon; so we have the incentive not only to economise in manpower generally against the background of finance and recruiting, but also, within the manpower we have, to ensure that as great a proportion as possible is in the fighting units and as small a proportion as possible in the units that support them. Against that background, as with the other services, manpower control is a continuing activity, and this is not an empty phrase because the disciplines are applied tightly throughout the Army in two forms. First of all, what I might call the standard establishment control procedure—the means of periodic inspection of units and the examination of establishment by establishment committees—and secondly by an annual review carried out by a standing committee under the Army Board, which looks at the requirement for manpower as a whole over the period ahead, and applies cuts necessary to ensure that the total is a reasonable one. These standard procedures are supplemented from time to time by special projects and in the paper we have given four examples of which the Stainforth Committee is a good one because it did produce major savings in one particular area. Whether and when projects of that kind are undertaken does depend on the circumstances at the time and the opportunities which present themselves. Is there a command organisation in the United Kingdom which would yield to examination and produce savings? It was thought at the time of the Stainforth Committee there was such an opportunity and it was taken. Similarly, with the introduction of computerisation this was looked at, at the time it was thought right to do so, and the reorganisation of the junior training similarly. It is true that we have not undertaken in the time scale we are talking about a comprehensive study of the kind undertaken by the Royal Air Force, but, as Mr. Herd has said, the Defence Review is now opening up a new situation in which a comprehensive examination will be necessary.

Chairman.] I would like to thank you all for coming and giving your interesting evidence to us this afternoon. I think it has been very worth while. Thank you.

APPENDIX 1

TRAINING—SUPPLEMENTARY QUESTIONS (D.15)

Memorandum by the Ministry of Defence

1. This Memorandum contains answers to questions 2, 4, 5, 6, 7 and 8 posed by the Sub-Committee as a result of evidence taken on training on 18th June, 1974. The remaining answers will follow at a later date.

Basis adopted for comparison of the syllabi offered as Appendices to SCOE 31/9/2/2

2. The syllabi are those in use by the Services now and are designed to meet specific training objectives. Each syllabus is kept under regular review to ensure that it meets current requirements. Comparison of the syllabi one with another with a view to standardisation would flow only from rationalisation of training objectives on which subject separate evidence has been and is being given to the Sub-Committee. In these circumstances the Ministry of Defence approach has been to regard comparison of the syllabi as meaningful only in the context of training objectives and the Services' requirements for the skills in question.

Savings achieved by the computerisation of pay and personnel records on each of the Services

3. Each computer project receives financial approval on the basis of a 10-year costing forward from the start of a project. Quantifiable savings do arise from the substitution of machines for personnel, but it is not possible to be entirely precise in expressing the manpower savings achieved because of the substantial time span of development of projects, during which changes in requirements arise. The order of savings, which can be substantiated, as regards the Services' pay and personnel systems in terms of staff numbers (uniformed and civilian) is as follows:

HMS Centurion	150
RAPC Worthy Down	650 (plus a further 90 from 1975–76 resulting from a further stage of the system).
RAF Innsworth	600

4. Very large savings were achieved with the introduction of the first generation of computers. At that stage effort was concentrated on straight transfer of manual systems to automatic data processing methods. Thereafter, with experience and greater appreciation of the potentialities of ADP and in preparation for the next generation of more sophisticated machines, attention was turned to improving the pay and record systems. This was through single Service rationalisation, streamlining procedures and redesigning forms to achieve savings in staff as well as enhancing the service to personnel, management and manpower planning. Examples of improvements made are the payment through bank accounts of a large proportion of soldiers and airmen, the use of microfilm for record storage, and fuller and more consistent routine provision of information for such purposes as man-power management.

5. Of the savings in recent years it is not possible to distinguish between those attributable to the greater capacity and capability of the computers now used, and those resulting from improvements in procedures and rationalisation. Moreover, as explained in paragraph 4 above, a better service has been provided in spite of the smaller numbers employed.

Rationalisation of pay and personnel records in the Services—involvement of Civil Service Department

6. The major rationalisation of Service pay and personnel records within the individual Services in recent years has been connected with the introduction of computers. The CSD, and before them the Treasury, have always been involved in any proposal of this nature. This involvement extends not only to the evaluation and choice of the computer in question but also to the scrutiny of the systems that precede its introduction.

7. The CSD maintain a Management Services Division which is available to other Government Departments for consultation, and advice on the conduct of business. Larger Government Departments—such as the Ministry of Defence—however maintain their own Management Services organisation. The CSD would not expect to be called upon by these departments except upon some rather specialised issue such as the employment of a consultant or the introduction of a new management technique. Apart therefore from their substantial involvement in the introduction of computers in the Service pay and records field, the CSD have not been asked to advise. The Management Services Division of the Ministry of Defence have participated fully in all work in the MOD connected with Service pay and records and this will continue. Neither the CSD nor the MOD Management Services organisation have been specifically asked to advise on Service training which is primarily a matter for the Service authorities, except as regards ADP training. Civilian and uniformed Service ADP staff working in administrative areas (such as pay and records systems) are trained to common standards, the majority at Defence ADP training centres, augmented by Civil Service College and commercial facilities. The pattern of training currently being followed was promulgated by CSD following the recommendations of an inter-Departmental working party chaired by CSD and on which MOD was represented.

8. The Services were amongst the leaders in Britain in introducing computer-based pay and record systems. As a result there are many trained systems analysts, computer programmers and qualified accountants in the Services who have been responsible for designing the existing pay and records systems and in fact the Civil Service Department employ some of the Service experts in the management services and training fields.

9. The normal rules on inter-departmental consultation ensure that the CSD are kept aware of major issues, and they are asked to advise on subjects on which the MOD considers they would be of assistance.

Reasons for the training of drivers by the Services and not by civilian contract

10. Basic driver training is only some 25 per cent. of the courses for Service driver training. Servicemen are given instruction, for example, on mechanical principles, first-line vehicle maintenance, accident procedure, and recovery procedures ; they are also trained in the relevant operational skills such as camouflage and concealment drills, convoy discipline, daily vehicle maintenance, airfield driving, and are given skid-pan experience.

11. Moreover, within the field of basic training, commercial civilian driving schools are not geared to the provision of large scale continuous training. They exist to meet the civilian demand for spare time instruction. Any company that might be interested in large contracts would need to recruit staff and set up special facilities for Service requirements, which would lead to the dispersal of the Service teams of instructors, who would be extremely difficult to reassemble if, for example, the company decided not to continue the contract.

12. The Services doubt whether the quality of training given by civilian firms matches that given by the MOD. Even allowing for the fact that all Service trainees are young and fit, whilst civilian trainees are taken from a cross-section of the community as a whole, that Servicemen train continuously whilst civilians train sporadically, and that in the Services timing of testing is in the hands of the instructor, the failure rate of civilians who take the DOE test (about 54 per cent.) is unacceptably high for Service requirements.

13. As instruction given by a civilian firm would be exclusively in driving, military training needs, therefore, such as tactical handling, camouflage and daily vehicle maintenance, would have to be taught separately by Service Staff. Since the successful training of a Service driver depends upon the careful attention to elementary driving skills coupled closely with the associated military skills, this division of instruction between civilian contractors and MOD staffs would detract from efficient training.

14. Under our existing training arrangements we can ensure that a trainee is taught by the same Instructor throughout the course. Experience shows that this results in a valuable relationship building up which is a very good influence for discipline, particularly since so many of our trainees are very young. No outside contractor could play a similar part and the instructional staff concerned would not be part of the Service Unit nor under the control of the Commanding Officer.

15. All Service drivers are conditioned to being responsible for the routine maintenance of their vehicles. Civilian driving schools do not normally implant this idea into their trainees, because their successful pupils do not need to be responsible for the maintenance of their vehicles.

16. These reasons led to a decision being taken that the limitations imposed on the training programmes by placing driving training to civilian contract would be unacceptable to the MOD.

Failure rates of trainee vehicle drivers

17. The following statement shows the failure rate at the various levels of training for trainee vehicle drivers during 1973–74:—

	Service	Numbers commenced training	Numbers failing test—suspended prior to test and not completing course for other reasons e.g. voluntary discharge	Percentage failure rate
BASIC DRIVER TRAINING ...	RM ...	144	23	16
	Army ...	4,517	662	15
	RAF ...	381	36	10
UPGRADING TO CLASS 3 ...	RM ...	71	11	15
	Army ...	3,075	316	10
	RAF ...	376	54	14
UPGRADING TO CLASS 1 (A considerable element of this course is devoted to providing for administrative duties).	RM ...	7	Nil	—
	Army ...	729	46	6
	RAF ...	249	57	23

18. Since at the basic training stage all Service trainees are young able bodied men it has not been considered necessary to introduce a formal aptitude test although all three Services assess the general ability of the recruits prior to undertaking driver training. Lack of eye and muscle co-ordination is the most common cause of failure and is usually only confirmed after about one week of practical driving.

Failure rates of trainee rotary wing pilots

19. The process of selecting from pilot applications those considered suitable for training involves an aptitude test, medical examination and interviews. Aptitude testing for all three Services takes place at the Officer and Aircrew Selection Centre (OASC), RAF Biggin Hill.

20. Candidates take six tests for pilot aptitude. These cover general intelligence, the comprehension of mechanical diagrams and instruments, powers of co-ordination and anticipation and the capacity to keep track of constantly changing information. The tests were originally developed on the basis of psychological theory and all but one of them (that for general intelligence) were designed

specifically for Service use. Their continuing acceptance in use is always being re-assessed against performance in training and the candidates' score for each test is "weighted" by a factor derived from the usefulness that test has been found to have in predicting success in training.

21. It has been found over many years of use that the higher a candidate's pilot score, the more likely he is to be successful in flying training. There is a lower score limit below which no candidate is accepted for pilot training because his chances of success are such that he would not be considered an acceptable training risk. About 72 per cent of applicants reach the minimum standard whilst under 1 per cent achieve the maximum marks. At the lower end of the scale, over 50 per cent wastage rates could be expected in training if they went forward. The cut off line can be adjusted upwards, and in establishing the qualifying scores for entry to training, the Services take into account the numbers of people likely to apply for entry, the level of training wastage tolerated, and the number of trained men required. Selection policy is therefore determined by all these various interests.

22. The following is a statement of the failure rate of trainee rotary wing pilots during the year 1973–74:—

Service				Numbers commenced training	Failures	Percentage failure rate
RN	...	...	...	...	60	7	12
Army	...	...	...	...	66	12	20
RAF	...	...	...	...	16[1]	Nil	—

[1] During 1973–74 insufficient front line pilots' posts were available to absorb the planned output and therefore five courses were cancelled to avoid an excessively large number of pilots who had completed RW training and were awaiting conversion courses.

23. All three Services adopt a similar investigation procedure, leading to a trainee pilot being suspended during RW training, whereby the trainee is given the opportunity to improve his standard through extra instruction under close observation. Should the trainee continue to fall below the required standard he is examined by a special Board who make recommendations for his future employment.

24. Having investigated and interviewed each pilot who has failed during training, all three Services maintain a careful record of the reasons for failure and these records are constantly analysed to determine whether there are any recurring factors leading to failure, and whether they could be eliminated by an adjustment to the aptitude test.

August, 1974.

APPENDIX 2

TRAINING—SUPPLEMENTARY QUESTIONS (D18)

Memorandum by the Ministry of Defence (SCOE 31/9/2/4)

1. This Memorandum contains answers to questions 3, 9, 10 and 11 posed by the Sub-Committee as a result of oral evidence taken on training.

Question 3

Numbers of cooks, and certain other grades, trained annually to B1 in the Army—prospects of introducing unified training at this level.

2. As there are differences in advanced training requirements and methods the information is given below separately by trade. The figures given relate to the year 1973–74.

COOKS

3. The number of cooks trained to advance standards were as follows:—

RN/WRNS ...	...	...	...	...	91
RM ...	...	...	...	...	5
Army ...	...	...	...	...	253
RAF ...	...	...	...	...	8

Prospects of Unified Advanced Training

4. The content of the courses for the advanced training of cooks in all the Services covers similar ground so unification would not be difficult from this aspect alone. There would however be the problem of where such training could be carried out. The RN and Army schools are already at full capacity and, although RAF Hereford is at present temporarily under-utilised and could probably accommodate the numbers involved, such an arrangement could be only a short term expedient. To accommodate the unified advanced training of cooks on a permanent basis could therefore involve additional capital cost of building new domestic and technical accommodation in the longer term.

5. Even if the advanced training of cooks could be concentrated at one location, it is difficult to see that any substantial economy would result among establishments now engaged in the training of cooks. Advanced cook training is only a relatively small element of the establishments' task and its removal would not greatly reduce the overall administration costs. HMS PEMBROKE for instance. in addition to running many other courses, provides support facilities for Fleet Maintenance Group, Craft Maintenance Support, Reserve Ships and the Staff of the FO Medway ; RAF Hereford, in addition to accommodating the RAF School of Cooking is the initial training centre for WRAF recruits as well as the main training centre for secretarial and supply trades ; and the Army Catering Corps Training Centre at St. Omer Barracks Aldershot was built to meet the training requirements of students in Service catering for the Army as a whole. The removal of the B1 students from Aldershot would leave empty kitchen classrooms and reduce the food and meal production which is used to feed all the personnel at the Centre.

6. There is already close co-operation between the RM and the Army on advanced cookery training. The RN have for some time now attended a Supply course, a Catering Instructors course and a Butchery Duties course run by the Army Catering School, Aldershot.

CLERKS AND PAY CLERKS

7. The numbers of clerks and pay clerks trained to advanced standards were as follows: —

						Clerks	Pay Clerks
RN	...	...	...	...	...	46 (Writers)	
RM	...	...	...	...	...	5	4
Army	...	...	...	...	...	250	164([1])
RAF	...	...	...	...	...	'B1' standard is achieved during basic training.	

Prospects of Unified Advanced Training

8. At present pay clerks and clerks in the Services work in systems using terminology, documentation and procedures which differ widely between the Services, because of their different operational environments. A Royal Navy writer would not easily understand the system used by a Royal Air Force clerk accounting, nor that used by the Royal Army Pay Corps. Consequently, the unification of training of pay clerks is not at present practicable([2]).

VEHICLE MECHANICS

9. The numbers of vehicle mechanics trained to advanced standards were as follows: —

RM	...	...	...	...	...	4
Army	...	...	...	...	...	580
RAF	...	...	...	...	...	50

Prospects of Unified Advanced Training

10. One of the conclusions of the Defence Training Committee Working Party([3]) was that SEME([4]) Bordon had the capacity and ability to devise tailor-made vehicle mechanic courses for the RM and RAF. The Defence Training Committee tasked the Army with investigating further the advantages and disadvantages of co-locating all vehicle mechanic training at SEME Bordon. The result of this further study is expected to be available towards the end of 1974.

DRIVERS

11. The numbers of drivers trained to advanced standards were as follows:

RM	...	...	...	...	...	9
Army	...	...	...	...	...	683
RAF	...	...	...	...	...	249

Prospects of Unified Advanced Training

12. Upgrading courses to B1 standard for fully qualified drivers in all the Services are usually carried out at units. It is considered that this sort of training can best be conducted in this way since it can be slotted into the man's normal working environment. No special training facilities have to be provided. For example, much of the upgrading course consists of administrative training in the motor

[1] Army Pay Clerks are trained for upgrading to B1 by internal correspondence course at their place of duty.

[2] The possibility of introducing common procedures for the Services is the subject of a separate note to the Sub-Committee.

[3] This is the subject of a separate note to the Sub-Committee. (Appendix 3).

[4] School of Electrical and Mechanical Engineering

transport field, e.g. convoy organisation, handling of forms and knowledge of procedures associated with requisitioning transport. Another element in these courses may be specialist training on vehicles peculiar to one Service or branch of Service. These again are available on the unit.

13. Where it is practicable to do so, training is carried out on a joint basis—the main example being a conversion course for HGV drivers which is run by the Army. In general the means of giving instruction in these matters are readily available at unit level, avoid the costs which would be involved in the setting up of a central establishment and keep to a minimum the disturbance normally associated with attendance at some central establishment.

Question 9

Details of progress made on unification of training of ancillary medical staff; of medical assistants; and of male nurses at the higher levels.

14. A statement of the training of nursing and medical and dental ancillary personnel at present carried out on a joint basis is set out at Annex A to this Memorandum.

15. The Jarrett Committee concluded that too many small, separate establishments for training special technical skills ancillary to medicine were being maintained by the Services; and they identified those areas in which they considered there should be further rationalisation, namely the training of physiotherapists, radiographers, laboratory technicians, dental hygienists and dental technicians. The recommendations of the Jarrett Committee are set out at Annex B to this Memorandum.

Training of Physiotherapists, Radiographers and Laboratory Technicians (Jarrett Recommendations 56, 59 and 60)

16. Studies within the ambit of the Defence Medical Services Co-ordinating Committee have indicated that it would be physically feasible to set up tri-Service schools to train uniformed physiotherapists, radiographers and laboratory technicians, but some professional penalties might well be incurred by any single-Service medical organisation losing its own single-Service school. The loss of civilian recognition for the training is considered unlikely but would be dependent upon the approval of the tri-Service schools by the professional bodies concerned. Concentration of the training might not, however, in every case be achieved without additional capital expenditure or necessarily produce overall savings in trained technicians.

17. These Jarrett Committee recommendations are now being examined to assess any additional capital costs and the overall effects on running costs and manpower that would result from their implementation. The appropriate civilian professional bodies will also need to be consulted before any final decisions are taken.

Training of Dental Hygienists (Jarrett Recommendation 57)

18. The Defence Medical Services Co-ordinating Committee have concluded that this recommendation by the Jarrett Committee would not be feasible because:

(a) The training requires access to patients and there would be insufficient Service patients to satisfy the requirements of a combined school at Halton or in either of the areas in which the other two Services' schools are situated.

(b) Concentration would produce no saving in tutorial staff and would require increases in fully trained hygienists by the RN and Army at Portsmouth and Aldershot respectively to compensate for the loss of work performed by trainee hygienists.

(c) Additional domestic and instruction accommodation would be needed at Halton for the combined task.

Training for Dental Technicians (Jarrett Recommendation 58)

19. The Army enters trained or partially trained dental technicians as well as untrained men for this trade and they are all trained as part of the Army's Adult

Training Scheme; the RAF entry into this trade is restricted to untrained recruits who undergo a full apprentice training. This and other differences in training requirements between the two Services make their approaches to dental technician training incompatible. Furthermore there is insufficient accommodation at Halton (or for that matter at the new Army training establishment at Aldershot) to meet the needs of a joint school without a costly rebuilding programme. For these reasons it has been concluded that the training of Service dental technicians should not be amalagmated at Halton as recommended in the Jarrett Report. The respective costs of dental technician training in the Army and RAF are, however, being examined and the results of this may point the way to possible changes which will bring the two Services closer together in their approaches to this training.

Male Nurses and Medical Assistants

20. The Jarrett Committee have made no specific recommendations relating to the joint training of medical grades beyond those discussed in paragraphs 14 to 17 above; and it is upon these specific recommendations that the Defence Medical Services Co-ordinating Committee have concentrated their attention in regard to the further training of medical grades.

21. The further clinical training of male nurses is provided primarily by "on the job" training in Service hospitals or by secondment to civilian hospitals or courses organised by other outside bodies. Management training for nursing staff is provided by courses with non-Service institutions; courses at the QARANC Training Centre, Aldershot, or Service run management courses where the students are taken from other branches of the Services besides the Medical Services. The courses at the QARANC Training Centre are at present confined to commissioned officers so far as male nurses are concerned.

22. The Navy and Army have medical assistants while the RAF has two distinct grades of State Enrolled Nurse and Medical Secretarial. As explained in Memorandum SCOE/31/9/2, there is a wide disparity between the Services in the levels of training and the final qualification required to meet the individual requirements of the Services from these grades which militates against joint training for them.

23. The post registration training of male nurses and the training of medical assistants are not, therefore, fields in which further rationalisation might be expected.

Question 10

Examples of savings in training time achieved by the Royal Navy and the Army through the use of job analysis

24. In the Royal Navy the purpose of job analysis is to define the tasks which a man will carry out in the Fleet on completion of his training. These tasks will be in three categories:—

   (*a*) Those which he will be sure to carry out in any class of ship.

   (*b*) Those which he will carry out only in certain classes of ship or in those with unique equipment.

   (*c*) Those which he may occasionally carry out in any class of ship.

25. The present policy is that career courses will train a man for category 'A' task only. Category 'B' tasks are covered in separate courses, known as Pre-joining Training (PJT) and given only to those ratings drafted to certain ships. Category 'C' tasks are taught after the man has joined his ship: this is known as OJT (On Job Training).

26. This new concept, known as Objective Training, of which job analysis is an essential component, was introduced in 1971 and replaced the original philosophy that career training should prepare all men for category 'A', 'B' and 'C' tasks. There are three levels of job analysis in use in the Royal Navy:—

    (a) CODAP—a new, formal process which relies on computer processing to analyse a questionnaire specially prepared for each analysis.

    (b) NMUU Analysis—carried out by specially trained officers and ratings from the Naval Manpower Utilisation Unit.

    (c) In House Analysis—carried out on a subjective basis by the staff of the professional schools, sometimes assisted by NMUU.

27. In the Army, Job Analysis is but one part of what is termed the Systems Approach to Training, a continuous cycle of events which aims at achieving both greater efficiency and greater effectiveness in training. The Systems Approach is the basis on which all individual training is designed and reviewed in the Army today and is implemented through the medium of Training Development Teams (TDTs) in each of the major Arms and Services. Specialist Training Development Advisers are found in the TDTs and at the Army School of Instructional Technology (ASIT).

28. Job analysis can of course result in either the identification of a need for revised or additional training, or the identification of unnecessary training. It has been the Army's experience that the increasing complexity of modern equipment and techniques has increased the diversity of skills required of the individual soldier to such a degree that, all too often, the result of job analysis is a demand for extra training. Only by balancing such demands against the realities of limited time and resources has the increase in length of many courses been avoided.

29. Despite this aspect, job analysis and the systems approach continue to be widely used: and the systems approach with its disciplined and objective techniques enable the Army to be quite clear as to their individual training needs when deciding how to make the best use of time, resources and manpower. Recently the CODAP process used in the Royal Navy was presented to Army personnel and as a result steps have been taken to have this technique examined further.

30. Examples of savings achieved as a result of job analysis are set out in the following tables:—

ROYAL NAVY

School (1)	Course (2)	Old Course Length (3)	New Course Length (4)	Annual Throughput (Student/Years) (5)	Annual Saving in Training Time (Student/Weeks) (6)
HMS MERCURY	Leading Radio Operator (Tactical) ...	14 weeks	9 weeks	83	415
HMS DRYAD	Radar Plotter First-Class	17 weeks	13 weeks	64	256
HMS PHOENIX	NBCD[1] General	10 days	8 days	500	200
HMS SULTAN	Ship Husbandry—Junior Ratings	5 days	3 days	375	150
HMS COLLINGWOOD ...	Ordnance Electrical Mechanics—Qualifying	12 weeks	11 weeks	350	350

1 Nuclear, Biological and Chemical Defence.

D 4

Sponsor Arm/Service (1)	Course (2)	Old Course Length (3)	New Course Length (4)	Annual Throughput (Student/Year) (5)	Annual Saving in Training Time (Student/Weeks) (6)
RAC	Driver—Army Fighting Vehicles:				
	Chieftain	7 weeks 2 days	3 weeks 4 days	149	536
ROYAL SIGNALS	Combat Linesman:				
	Class 3	11 weeks	8 weeks	67	201
	Class 1	9 weeks	5 weeks	37	148
	Telecommunication Mechanic:				
	Class 3	36 weeks	33 weeks	50	150
	Class 1	20 weeks	16 weeks	5	20
ROYAL CORPS OF TRANSPORT ...	Squadron Sergeant Major's Course	8 weeks	5 weeks	48	144
	Radio Operators (Classes 3 and 2)	14 weeks	9 weeks	66	330
					237
	Port Employments:				
	Freight Handler Stevedore:				
	Class 3	6 weeks	See Terminal Despatcher	26	
	Class 2	7 weeks		14	See note over.
	Class 1	8 weeks		8	
	Heavy Crane Operator:				
	Class 3	13 weeks	See Terminal Operator	15	
	Class 2	6 weeks		14	
	Class 1	6 weeks		3	

(1) Sponsor Arm/Service	(2) Course	(3) Old Course Length	(4) New Course Length	(5) Annual Throughput (Student/Year)	(6) Annual Saving in Training Time (Student/Weeks)
ROYAL CORPS OF TRANSPORT ...	**Terminal Despatcher:**				(Re-organisation—6 levels of training reduced to 4 levels).
	Class 3 ...	⎫ Previously Freight Handler Stevedore and Heavy Crane Operator ⎬	3 weeks	15	
	Terminal Operator:				
	Class 3 ...		5½ weeks	19	
	Class 2 ...		6 weeks	32	
	Class 1 ...	⎭	3 weeks	12	
	Maritime Deck Employments:			Old / New	
	Seaman:				242
	Class 3 ...	11 weeks	10 weeks	56 / 26	
	Class 2 ...	6 weeks	6 weeks	33 / 19	
	Class 1 ...	6 weeks	—	5 / —	(Re-organisation—7 levels of training reduced to 5 levels).
	Navigator:				
	Class 3 ...	12 weeks	14 weeks	31 / 56	
	Class 2 ...	9 weeks	8 weeks	22 / 13	
	Class 1 ...	10 weeks	5 weeks	9 / 3	
	Navigator (T) Class 1 ...	5 weeks		3 / 3	

Sponsor Arm/Service (1)	Course (2)	Old Course Length (3)	New Course Length (4)	Annual Throughput (Student/Year) (5)	Annual Saving in Training Time (Student/Weeks) (6)
REME[1]	*Metal Worker Employments:*				351
	Fitter Gun:				(Some 50 posts were eliminated in the re-organisation.)
	Class 3	27½ weeks	—	45	
	Class 1	7 weeks	—	24	
	Fitter Gun (AFV):				
	Class 3	—	31 weeks	24	
	Class 1	—	9 weeks	12	
	Fitter Gun (Field):				
	Class 3	—	26¼ weeks	24	
	Class 1	—	11½ weeks	12	
	Armourer:			*Old* *New*	
	Class 3	28 weeks	31 weeks	60 70	
	Class 1	10 weeks	8 weeks	24 25	
	Fitter Turner:				
	Class 3	33 weeks	—	30	
	Class 1	4 weeks	—	8	
RAOC	All Arms Clerks Course: upgrading B2—B1	25 days	11·3 days	349	956
RAPC/WRAC	Clerk (WRAC): Classes 3 and 2	9 weeks	8 weeks	69	69 (Exclusive of on the job training now eliminated.)
APTC	All Arms: Assistant Instructor in PT	13 weeks	9 weeks	*Old* 216 / *New* 320	−72 (but major increase in throughput)

[1] It will be observed that in some cases the length of the course has been increased. Nevertheless, the re-organisation of the group of employments and the elimination of certain training courses has resulted in the overall saving in training time as set out in Column 6.

Question 11

Why Service pay and personnel documents have been rationalised on a single-Service Basis

31. The primary source of all information needed to administer Service pay and records is the ship or unit. The process must start when either the man notifies his ship or unit about, or the ship or unit records, a change in his circumstances, which affects his pay, allowances or charges, or otherwise requires an amendment to central records.

32. The three Services are of necessity organised on different lines. The Royal Air Force mainly consists of large establishments at fixed locations. The Army includes both large and small units, many of which frequently move at short notice on operations and training to temporary locations. The Royal Navy has to administer personnel in large and small ships, and in shore establishments. The different roles and consequent type of organisation in each of the three Services result in varying degree of movement of personnel. In particular, much larger numbers of Navy and Army personnel have to serve away from their headquarters or base than is normal in the RAF.

33. Because all pay and records documentation starts in the ship or unit, it is more efficient to use systems specially adapted to the practical needs of each Service. In large units, it is a practical proposition to employ pay, accounts and records staff at the unit ; and so it is possible to decentralise as much documentation as possible to the units, where the information originates, and to make adjustments at once when the circumstances of an individual change. By comparison, in a small ship or unit it is not feasible to employ pay, accounts and records staff to the same extent ; it follows that pay and records documentation has to be centralised at a headquarters or base.

34. However, there are other considerations. For example, while payment through a bank account is the most acceptable and efficient means of issuing pay to Officers and Other Ranks who are stationed in areas having adequate local banking facilities, it is not so practical for men at sea, or serving in remote areas. An efficient Service pay and records system must be able to cope with Service personnel in inaccessible and temporary locations where it is not practical to employ pay and records personnel to administer them, and it has to be designed for use in war as well as peace. If there were a single system for all three Services, it would have to provide for the whole range of large units, minor units, ships at sea, men in the jungle, and so on ; and the result might well be the creation of more than three different sub-systems, to meet the whole range of possible circumstances.

35. It is true that entitlement to pay and allowances, and liability for charges, are so far as possible made identical in the three Services ; but many other terms, conditions and regulations which have a bearing on pay are dissimilar, notably lengths of engagements of Servicemen, the special sea-going arrangements in the Royal Navy and the different types of commissions in the three Services. The existing single Service pay and records systems, which must take account of these differences, are necessarily complex ; a tri-Service system might well add more complications to the procedural instructions which now have to be followed in units and ships.

36. A further point is that information from the personnel records on the single Service computers are used *inter alia* in connection with career planning, promotions, identifying training requirements, and posting or drafting of personnel. The methods of career planning, rules for promotion, and training needs differ between the three Services, as does to a lesser extent posting and drafting e.g. in the Navy and RAF people tend to move as individuals whereas often in the Army they move as units. The main differences in the career planning, promotion and training fields spring from basic Service organisation and mean that a single set of records, unified on a tri-Service basis, could not have been used for these purposes.

37. For all these reasons the work of improving pay and record systems developed on a single Service basis, and the process of introducing ADP systems, together with the capacity of the computers at the time, dictated this approach. The possibility of removing differences between the three Service systems, as far as the basic situation allows, is kept under active consideration.

Why separate computers are operated for this purpose

38. The reasons for this are two-fold. Firstly, differences between the pay-systems and management record-keeping requirements of the Services. Secondly, differences arising from the history and time-span of the computerisation of pay and records in each Service as summarised in the following table:

	Project Started	Computer Ordered	Computer Delivered	Replacement Date
RAPC WORTHY DOWN First Project: 1 No. IBM 360/30, 2 No. IBM 705, 1 No. IBM 1401.	November 1955	September 1958	October 1960	1970–71
Second (Replacement) Project: 1 No. IBM 360/50 ... ... + 1 No. IBM 360/50 ... ... Second machine subsequently replaced by an IBM 370/158.	May 1966	June 1969	July 1970 August 1971 March 1974	1979–80
RAF INNSWORTH 1 No. Univac 1107	1957	1963	1965	1976
HMS CENTURION 1 No. ICL 1904E	August 1963	August 1967	June 1969	1978–79

39. Prior to mid-1970 general purpose computers were of limited size; in particular there were constraints on the provision of capacity for handling complex tasks with large data bases. The payroll for officers and men in the Armed Services was then of the order of 350,000. Nevertheless a long and exhaustive study was undertaken in 1965 of the possibilities of accommodating the Navy task on the RAF's Univac 1107. The study found that this was not practicable. However, features of the system approach of the RAF were adopted beneficially by HMS CENTURION.

Whether it is intended to replace the existing computers with one installation to take all Service Pay etc records

40. The RAF System is the first due to be replaced and negotiations on a single tender basis, are presently in hand with ICL for a New Range machine. A study of the HMS CENTURION replacement is about to get under way and one possibility that will be closely examined is that of carrying out the task on a further New Range machine which, as a large bureau (Bureau West), will provide the computing capacity for a number of Defence management systems. This is due for delivery in mid-1975 subject to an order being placed shortly; negotiations are in hand with ICL. These two New Range machines will be compatible. When the Worthy Down replacement is considered, a machine of the ICL New Range will be a candidate.

41. Thus the aim is computer compatibility, with attendant benefits including the availability of alternative computing resources in an emergency, rather than provision of one installation for three separate pay and records systems. The replacement requirements for all Defence management systems currently using dedicated computer facilities are being reviewed in the context of the possibility that they might eventually be combined in a small number of major bureaux,

and this will at the appropriate time take into account the replacement planning for the Services' pay and records systems.

What arrangements exist for examination of the possibility of unifying Service pay, etc, records and what timetable has been fixed for this

42. The Ministry of Defence has appointed a committee with expert representatives from the three Services to review the pay and records systems of the Services and to consider the extent to which they might be developed on similar lines, compatible with the individual requirements of the three Services to pay and record information.

43. The system of determining rates of Service pay, allowances and charges ensures that these are common to all three Services; thus, each Report of the Armed Forces Pay Review Body deals with all three Services together, and fixes the rates for each Service alongside the others. Similarly, when the rules of entitlement to a new payment are drawn up, or the rules for an existing payment are revised, a single formula is worked out to apply to all three Services. It follows that except for a few comparatively minor details, the intended entitlement to pay and allowances, and liability for charges, does not differ between the three Services. Action is being taken in the normal course to abolish any differences which are not justified by special conditions in a particular Service.

44. However, though entitlement is to all intents and purposes identical, it is essential that the people who have to issue the pay and allowances and to make the charges in the service units should understand the position thoroughly. The paying authorities are of course remote from headquarters and it is important to recognise the risk of mistakes through misinterpretation at this level. To avoid this and to clarify the position as much as possible, each Service has its own regulations with the aim of setting out the entitlement clearly in the context of the organisation and terminology of that service. The objections to producing a single set of regulations are:—

(*a*) different terms are used in the three Services for the same details e.g. ratings and ranks, posting and transfers.

(*b*) the application of a particular entitlement to the diverse situations encountered in the three Services e.g. at sea, at base, in the field etc requires independent sets of rules.

(*c*) the regulations are provided for use in ships and units and are already extremely complex, though we try to keep them as simple as possible. The inclusion of all the rules for all three Services in one volume might well complicate the regulations.

45. This does not mean that the single-Service regulations cannot be rationalised and improved. For example, as in all other aspects of Service administration, a standard language is being developed across the three Services for pay and records terms, and this should in time remove the difficulty at (*a*) above. Again, it is the methods of payment needed by each of the Services to meet their differing situations which have dictated the pay and records systems that each Service has evolved; and the MOD Committee are investigating methods of payment to see what rationalisation is possible, so that they can be developed on similar lines in all three Services.

46. No timetable had been fixed for unifying Service pay and records.
September 1974

ANNEX A TO SCOE 31/9/2/4

Question 9

JOINT TRAINING AT PRESENT BEING CARRIED OUT FOR MEDICAL GRADES

Mental Nurses

Students from all three Services are trained at the Army's Royal Victoria Hospital, Netley. RN and Army trainees are seconded to the RN Hospital, Haslar for the General Nursing part of their course.

Radiographers

Army and RAF personnel are trained at the Army School of Radiography, Woolwich.

Laboratory Technicians

RN medical technician trainees undergo a three year course of which the first 12 months are spent at the RAF Institute of Pathology and Tropical Medicine, Halton.

Dispensers

The initial six months training for trainees from all three Services is carried out at the Army School of Dispensing, Colchester followed by " on the job " training at selected hospitals.

Electro-physiological Technicians

ECG Recordists

Army personnel also attend these courses for RAF personnel at RAF Hospital, Wroughton.

Obstetric Course

QARNNS personnel attend these courses held at the Military Maternity Hospital, Woolwich and BMH Rinteln.

Art of Examining

Middle Management

Courses in these subjects at the QARANC Training Centre are also attended by students from the RN and RAF Medical Services.

Clinical Measurements

The RAF provide this training for both RAF and Army nurses at the Central Medical Establishment.

Remedial Gymnast

This training is undertaken for all three Services at the Joint Service Rehabilitation Unit, Chessington under the guidance of the RAF School of Physiotherapy.

Radiological Protection

Courses in Radiological Protection are held at the Institute of Naval Medicine, Alverstoke at which personnel from all three Services attend.

ANNEX B TO SCOE 31/9/2/4

Question 9

JOINT TRAINING OF MEDICAL GRADES—RECOMMENDATIONS MADE BY THE JARRETT COMMITTEE

Recommendation 54.   Since the Services maintain too many small, separate establishments for specialist trade training, a drive should be made to rationalise as many of them as possible: meanwhile individual Services should not incur expenditure on facilities which may prove nugatory.

Recommendation 55.   When training establishments are rationalised, it will naturally be convenient for each to be run by a single-Service as appropriate. Members of all Services, however, particularly instructors should have the opportunity of being posted to them.

Recommendation 56. The three single-Service schools of physiotherapy should be replaced by a tri-Service school and full account should be taken of the views of the Physiotherapists' Board in selecting its future location and method of operation.

Recommendation 57. All training of dental hygienists should be concentrated in the RAF Dental Training Establishment at Halton.

Recommendation 58. All dental technicians should be trained at the RAF Dental Training Establishment at Halton.

Recommendation 59. A single school of radiographers should be set up. It should be located at, or in the vicinity of, the Naval Hospital at Haslar.

Recommendation 60. A single centre for the theoretical training of laboratory technicians should be set up. It should be located at the Royal Army Medical College, Millbank, if practicable.

APPENDIX 3

TRAINING (D.19)

Memorandum by the Ministry of Defence (SCOE 31/9/2/5) (D.19)

1. The Sub-Committee has asked for a paper about the Defence Training Committee Working Party (DTCWP) on the Joint Training of Servicemen showing:

(a) The Terms of Reference of the DTCWP ;

(b) The conclusions reached by the DTCWP ;

(c) The views of the Defence Training Committee (DTC) on the conclusions of the DTCWP ;

(d) Details of further studies commissioned, and the likely timescale for their completion.

2. The composition, Terms of Reference and method of working of the DTCWP are given in Annex A to this Memorandum ; details of their findings, conclusions and recommendations, together with the views of the DTC, are given by trades in Appendices 1-10 to Annex A.

3. We believe this analysis shows that while there are no objections to joint training as a matter of principle—and indeed we have never contended that there are —there are good reasons in practice why the scope of its application is limited. The main ones are:

(a) The Services' environment is an important element in basic training. Experience has shown that recruits want to be identified with the Service of their choice.

(b) It is Government policy to maintain separate Services. Many of the training requirements for these Services are different. For example, helicopter pilots in each of the Services do different jobs ; so also do pay clerks. The RN helicopter pilot flies mainly on anti-submarine missions over the sea ; the Army pilot is usually engaged on the tactical support of ground troops ; the RAF helicopter pilot is largely flying in the field of heavy logistic support. Pay clerks operate widely different systems in ships, on detached duty with Army units or in large fixed RAF installations. This means that in these areas training courses and instruction cannot be identical.

(c) Although common training for all three Services is sometimes in itself a more efficient form of training, and is pursued as a goal whenever suitable, the main argument in its favour is that it produces economies. The MOD capital investment in existing training land and buildings has already been made. Unless one Service can take over a complete training task for one or both of the others, thus allocating whole establishments to be closed, the institution of common training is unlikely to effect significant economies. Indeed it is likely to require capital expenditure for alterations to existing building or the provision of new ones.

4. It may be that as a result of the Defence Review, intakes at training establishments will be affected. Such a development may alter the balance of advantage and the question of the joint training of common administrative grades will therefore be examined in the light of the outcome of the Defence Review.

ANNEX A TO SCOE/31/9/2/5

REPORT BY THE DEFENCE TRAINING COMMITTEE WORKING PARTY (DTCWP) ON THE JOINT TRAINING OF SERVICEMEN

1. In 1973 the Principal Personnel Officers Committee instructed the Defence Training Committee to examine the methods, objectives, and location of training in the basic skills of certain trades within the Armed Services. The Defence Training Committee set up a Working Party of three Officers, one from each Service, i.e. Commander RN, Lieutenant-Colonel Army, and Wing Commander RAF. The group were independent of the single Service directorates, and were allowed about 4 months to work full time on the task. The terms of reference of the DTC Working Party were as follows:

(a) To examine the methods, objectives, and location of the initial training in the basic skill of the specialisation in the following categories in all three Services ;

    (1) *Priority 1*
        Cooks
        Helicopter Pilots
        Medical Orderlies
        Vehicle Mechanics
        Pay Clerks
        Clerical Staff
        Drivers

    (2) *Priority 2*
        Members of the Service Education Branches
        Service Police
        Dog Handlers
        Postal Service Personnel
        PT Instructors

(b) To analyse the extent to which training objectives in the three Services are common or similar ; and the reasons for such differences as do exist.

(c) To consider how far it would be practicable from the training view point to combine the training of more than one Service at a single location.

(d) Where combined training is considered practicable from the training view-point, to advise on the possible location of any such combined training ; and to give a general indication of any additional facilities, works services, etc. required.

(e) To report periodically to the Chairman, Defence Training Committee if this is felt desirable. In any event to report on Priority 1 categories by 31st December, 1973 and on Priority 2 categories by that date if practicable, or as soon as possible thereafter.

(f) In general terms, the initial training should be taken as the period during which the trainee is initiated into his trade/skill until he is available for his first posting as a trained man or to proceed to specialised single Service training. The parameters will vary with each function ; when in doubt the Working Party is to take guidance from the Chairman of the DTC.

2. Within the time available the DTCWP found it was unable to examine the priority 2 categories of Service Police and Dog Handlers.

Methodology

3. The DTCWP generally adopted the following method of work in its examination of the trades listed:

(a) A study of any available former rationalisation studies.

(b) Individual discussions by the DTCWP with the Service Departments and Specialist Officers in the Ministry of Defence.

(c) Visits to the appropriate Establishments to look at the training facilities and to discuss the general conduct of training.

(d) A DTCWP discussion to decide the general impression gained from the appreciation of the individual Service training methods, before coming to conclusions.

4. In the course of their examination of training methods the DTCWP visited 17 Service Training Stations and other Establishments. The Working Party's findings, conclusions, and recommendations are given by trade in the following appendices.

September 1974

COOKS

Method

1. The method of cook training is by formal classroom instruction followed by a period of supervised employment.

Objectives

2. The DTCWP found the training objectives of each Service for Cook training are as follows:

(a) *RN and RM*

To train RN entrants to a standard required to fill complement billets as Ordinary Ratings including up to 6 months supervised continuation training. RN Cooks who subsequently pass the Leading Cooks Course graduate at City and Guilds 706/1 level. Royal Marines also attend the basic course, followed by one week of field cookery. They are then qualified to fill an establishment post in a Command.

(b) *Army*

To train cooks to basic (B3) standard to feed the men of his Unit by preparing, cooking and serving food under supervision of an NCO or more qualified Cook. B3 tradesmen are under supervision for up to 6 months when they can qualify for City and Guilds London Institute Certificate 706/1 and regrading to B2.

(c) *RAF*

To train Cooks up to LAC standard to have the ability to use the equipment of the trade, and an elementary knowledge of duties, procedures, and documentation associated with the trade of Cook. LAC Cooks graduate at City and Guilds 706/1 level, but are still under supervision for about 6 months.

Locations

3. The team examined the facilities available for training at HMS Pembroke for the Navy and Royal Marines, Aldershot for the Army, and RAF Hereford. None of these establishments were found to have sufficient capability in the medium term to accommodate all the basic cookery training for the three Services, although the training of RN Cook Instructors is undertaken by the Army at Aldershot.

Training Plans

4. The DTCWP found there were plans under consideration for some changes in basic training;

(a) The RN and RM course is to be redesigned in detail but the scope and length of the course will remain the same.

(b) It has been recommended that the Army course be extended slightly (by one or two weeks) to give instruction on the preparation of some foods not at present in the syllabus[1].

(c) Proposals to reduce the RAF course to fourteen weeks[2] were being studied.

Conclusions

5. The DTCWP concluded that;

(a) With the exception of the abolition of Apprentice Cook training at RAF Hereford there have been no other fundamental changes in the RAF since 1968.

---

[1] Further study has indicated that, before the recommendation could be properly considered, it will be necessary to review the job specifications, training objectives, syllabuses and test standards at all craft levels.
[2] The RAF course has since been reduced to 14 weeks.

(b) Basic cookery training is broadly the same for all Services, but there are factors militating against the amalgamation of the training in one location at present.

(c) There are differences in the course lengths of the Army and RAF compared with the RN basic cookery course and these are related to the stated training objectives and the degree of supervision that is subsequently required.

(d) An RAF proposal to change to a new training pattern will reduce the training commitment at the basic stage and provide progressive training commensurate with advances in rank.

Recommendation

6. The DTCWP recommended that:

(a) Joint Service training of Cooks is not practicable whilst the single Service training objectives were dissimilar in the standards reached and the degree of supervision given to the cook in his first job.

(b) Since the craft of all cookery training is similar any future plans to relocate a single Service cookery training organisation should take into consideration any long term spare capacity which would enable a co-location of training organisations.

Views of the Defence Training Committee (DTC)

7. Although accepting that there was at first sight good general arguments for the co-location of basic cook training, the DTC considered that there was valid service reasons for the continuation of separate training, namely differing training objectives and loyalties.

APPENDIX 2 TO ANNEX A TO SCOE/31/9/25.

HELICOPTER PILOTS

Methods

1. The DTCWP summarised the training of the three Services which is all conducted on formal training courses as follows:

(a) RN

Navy Pilots are destined to fly helicopters only, but it has been found the preliminary training in flying fixed wing aircraft (FW) is invaluable in providing airmanship training, and is an inexpensive method of rejecting students, who show lack of flying aptitude, before the expensive helicopter (RW) phase of training is reached.

(b) Army

The Army's method is not dissimilar to that of the RN. Nearly all the students who enter flying training will, when later employed on operational flying duties, fly helicopters only. However the Army still has a small number of fixed wing operational aircraft and the basic fixed wing stage of flying training also serves as the first part of the course for those few students who are destined for fixed wing duties. As with the RN the basic FW stage also provides airmanship training and a filter process.

(c) RAF

All pilots are trained to 'wings' standard in fixed wing aircraft to permit a flexible policy for future employment of the pilots in FW aircraft or RW aircraft.

2. At the time the study took place the DTSWP found that the three Services used different aircraft, flown and maintained under dissimilar arrangements as follows:

(a) *RN*

The aircraft used by the RN were the Hiller and Whirlwind[1]. These aircraft were maintained under contract by a civilian firm.

(b) *Army*

Army helicopter flying training is based on the Bell 64 aircraft and is done under contract with a civilian firm in order to make the best use of the Army's limited aircrew manpower.

(c) *RAF*

The RAF use the Sioux[2] and Whirlwind[3] aircraft, flown and maintained by RAF personnel.

Objectives

3. The objective of each course of training is to bring the student to first pilot standard on an RW aircraft to enable him to go on to advanced and operational conversion training. Many of the exercises in the basic course are designed with the single service employment role in mind.

Locations

4. The DTCWP looked at facilities, air-space and buildings available at six Service Establishments and their five satellite or relief airfields. With the possible exception of the RAF helicopter flying training school at Tern Hill, Shropshire, none of the airfields at present in use could cope with the increased traffic which would result in colocation of all RW flying training. The DTCWP pointed out that before co-location could be considered in any strength the effect on the local environment would need careful study.

5. The DTCWP also studied the RN and Army primary FW flying, and the RN Commando and RAF Support Helicopter Training to see if there was any scope for rationalisation in these two aspects of training. The conclusions and recommendations below reflect this.

Conclusions

6. The DTCWP concluded that:

(a) No single Service organisation has the spare capacity in terms of hangars, accommodation, and air-space to accept another Services helicopter flying training requirement.

(b) While the RAF's policy is to train all pilots to 'wings' standard their objectives are incompatible with the RN and Army.

(c) RN and Army primary fixed wing training has similar objectives which may provide scope for rationalisation.

(d) The space capacity in the Army FW phase at Middle Wallop is insufficient to accept other than a small proportion of another Services task at present.

(e) Whilst the Services have large capital investments in existing equipment and aircraft it would be financially imprudent to introduce common equipment prematurely in order to promote a joint scheme of training.

(f) Although the only degree of similarity in the operational roles are those of the RN Commando and RAF Support Helicopter Pilots, there is a difference in their operational employment which precludes amalgamation or rationalisation at present.

(g) With the introduction of more sophisticated helicopters into Service, greater use should be made of procedure trainers and simulators, pooling resources as much as possible.

---

[1] To be replaced by the Gazelle in 1974.

[2] The Sioux has since gone out of service and training is now undertaken using the Whirlwind only.

[3] To be replaced by the Gazelle in 1974–75.

(*h*) Before considering the purchase of new types of training aircraft to perpetuate single Service training concepts, the Services should examine their requirements and objectives to determine where there is likely to be compatibility([1]).

(*j*) The individual Service Directorates are financially aware of the requirements to minimise training if only to commit more resources to be deployed in the front line.

(*k*) There is a requirement for all Services to review the full ramifications of an all-through([2]) helicopter training system, to determine if it is possible by this method to make significant financial savings without serious prejudice to the professional ability of the trained pilots.

Recommendations

7. The DTCWP recommended that:

(*a*) No changes should be introduced into the individual Service training methods in the short term ;

(*b*) The RN and Army should jointly investigate their future requirements for Fixed-Wing training to determine if there is scope for rationalisation and/or amalgamation in this phase ;

(*c*) The RN and RAF should, in the long term and in the light of changing requirements, review the operational training of Commando and Support Helicopter Pilots to determine if there is scope for an amalgamation and rationalisation of effort ;

(*d*) The three Services should give early attention to the full study of an all-through helicopter training, drawing on experience of civil industry as appropriate to compare the advantages and disadvantages of this system of training with existing ones ;

(*e*) Simulators and trainers should be more widely used in order to reduce training costs.

Views of the Defence Training Committee (DTC)

8. The DTC considered that arguments in favour of training within the chosen Service are not so compelling for pilots who are either Officers or, in the case of the Army, SNCOs with some maturity. However, the basic courses do contain exercises which have a direct bearing on later employment, and these early exercises within single Service training are of considerable value.

9. Finance, accommodation, and the effect on local communities, are important factors which have to be recognised. Co-location would not be feasible except possibly at RAF Tern Hill, but even there expensive works services would be required, the effect of increasing the air activity in that area by nearly $2\frac{1}{2}$ times would probably be unacceptable.

10. The DTC agreed that no changes should be made to helicopter pilot training in the short term but decided on further studies as follows:

(*a*) The RN should undertake a study on behalf of the RN and Army into the merits and logistics of the fixed-wing phase of training and report to the DTC.

(*b*) The RN should undertake a study on behalf of the RN and RAF into the merits of the rationalisation of the rotary-wing phase of Support Helicopter and Commando Flying and report to the DTC.

11. The results of these studies are expected to be available at the end of 1974 ; the DTC was opposed to the idea of an all-through Helicopter training course because pilots trained in this manner were found to have a lower standard of skill and took longer to reach operational competence than those with prior fixed wing

---

[1] No new plans are being considered for new training aircraft at present.

[2] All through helicopter training is a method whereby pilots are trained from the outset on helicopters and not given the benefit of prior fixed wing flying training.

experience. This decision was based on the Army's experience of an experimental all-through RW course; the Services could not be compared to civilian experience because military flying calls for a greater range of skills than those required for limited civilian roles, and it has been found that by giving a student pilot fixed-wing experience before embarking on the rotary-wing training was extremely valuable.

APPENDIX 3 TO ANNEX A TO SCOE/31/9/2/5

MEDICAL ORDERLIES

Introduction

1. The DTCWP found that the trade title of 'Medical Orderly' is no longer used by any of the Services to describe non-technical but highly skilled medical personnel employed by the three Services. The nearest equivalent titles are:

(*a*) *RN*

Medical Assistant.

(*b*) *Army*

RAMC Medical Assistant.

(*c*) *RAF*

Medical Secretarial/State Enrolled Nurse.

It is these trades which they examined in the context of joint training of 'Medical Orderlies'.

Objectives

2. Full descriptions of the differences in these trades were given to the Sub-Committee in SCOE/31/9/2, and the findings of the DTCWP confirmed the detail set out in that paper. The DTCWP reported that the Services basic training systems for 'Medical Orderlies' are very different and reflect the totally different 'end product' required by each Service to meet its operational needs. Inevitably therefore the time spent on basic training, the number of subjects and depth to which they are taught vary to a large extent and reflect different objectives, which are to train:

(*a*) *RN*

A highly skilled medical assistant who can work without supervision in a small ship without a doctor, with the sick and wounded often under harrowing conditions. He is also employed in Naval Hospitals and Medical Centres at home and abroad.

(*b*) *Army*

A medical assistant who can give immediate first-aid to a battlefield casualty and carry out the sustaining procedures required to hold the casualty for a limited period until he can arrange evacuation to a field hospital.

(*c*) *RAF*

A highly skilled nurse (SEN) and a medical administrator who jointly staff Medical Centres, and Service Hospitals in a static environment with, normally, a medical officer immediately available.

Conclusions

3. The DTCWP concluded that:

(*a*) whilst the three Services' objectives are so very different, no basis exists for joint training of 'Medical Orderlies';

(*b*) different methods of training with varying course lengths and content are justified by the individual Service requirements to train a tradesman for a particular operational role.

Recommendations

4. The DTCWP recommended that rationalisation and/or amalgamation of Service Medical personnel training is neither practicable nor necessary and should not be pursued.

Views of the Defence Training Committee (DTC)

5. The DTC recognised the need for each Service requiring totally different medical staff, and agreed with the recommendation of the Working Party, that as single Service training objectives are dissimilar joint training of personnel is neither desirable nor practicable.

APPENDIX 4 TO ANNEX A TO SCOE/31/9/2/5

VEHICLE MECHANICS

Method

1. The trade of Vehicle Mechanic is used in the Army and RM only, the RN has no requirement for Service personnel to maintain and repair vehicles. RN vehicles are repaired by MOD industrial civil servants. In the RAF the term Vehicle Mechanic comprises a two-part trade of MT Mechanic and MT Fitter. The methods of training carried out in all Services is by a formal training course.

Objectives

2. Training objectives in the services are:

   (a) *RM* To train a Marine to inspect, maintain, and carry out major repairs in the field to all Group B (soft skinned) vehicles held by a Commando. He is also trained to maintain and repair over-snow vehicles and outboard motors held by the RM.

   (b) *Army* To produce a Mechanic capable of employment in a Field Workshop, Light Aid Detachment, or as an attached Tradesman to a Field Force Unit. The mechanic is expected to play a full part in military activities in the field, normally working under supervision for six months but he has to be capable of working individually on the detached duty if required.

   (c) *RAF* To train an Airman as a Leading Aircraftsman MT Mechanic to carry out scheduled servicing, preventive maintenance and minor repairs of standard MT vehicles and their associated equipments. The RAF MT Mechanic would need to return for a further 23 weeks MT Fitter Course to achieve the same standard as the Army tradesman on graduation.

Locations

3. RM mechanics are trained by the Technical Training Company at RM Poole, this school has no spare capacity for training mechanics of the other services. Royal Air Force Mechanics are trained at RAF St. Athan which is fully committed to a number of other engineering courses. The Army train its Vehicle Mechanics at the School of Electrical and Mechanical Engineering at Bordon, Hants. The DTCWP found that SEME Bordon has the capacity to absorb all other Services vehicle mechanic training, and the ability to tailor courses to suit their needs.

Conclusions

4. The DTCWP concluded that:

   (a) the Army and RM training requirements are very similar. A common Vehicle Mechanic Training Course to suit both these Services could be devised ;

   (b) The RAF training objective is different from the other two Services and there is no common ground at this time ;

(c) the School of Electrical and Mechanical Engineering has the spare capacity to absorb all the 'Vehicle Mechanic' students from the other two Services if additional instructors and training equipments were established, and if minor works services to alter existing spare accommodation for instructional use were to be approved ;

(d) SEME Bordon has the ability to devise tailor-made courses to suit the RM and RAF training objectives ;

(e) both the RAF school at St. Athan and the Technical Training Company at Royal Marines, Poole, are working to full capacity and deal with other training and Station functions not connected with Vehicle Mechanic training. At both schools the training of Mechanics is linked functionally and economically with Driver training.

Recommendations

5. The DTCWP recommended that:

(a) no immediate change to the present single-Service training of Vehicle Mechanics is necessary ;

(b) the co-location of future training of Vehicle Mechanics at SEME Bordon should be investigated by the Army, RAF and the RM to identify actual costs, advantages and disadvantages.

Views of the Defence Training Committee (DTC)

6. The DTC noted that the report showed that SEME Bordon had the capacity and ability to devise tailor-made courses for the RM and RAF vehicle mechanics to suit single Service training objectives. It was decided that:

(a) The Army would investigate, on behalf of the RM, Army and RAF the possibility, costs, advantages and disadvantages, of co-locating all vehicle mechanic training at SEME Bordon.

7. The result of this further study is expected to be available by the end of 1974.

APPENDIX 5 TO ANNEX A TO SCOE/31/9/2/5

PAY CLERKS

Introduction

1. The DTCWP examined the trades of RN Writer, RM Clerk (Pay and Records), Royal Army Pay Corps Clerk, and RAF Clerk Accounting. The Committee found that although the employment to which all these Clerks go on graduation is similar, the syllabi used by the four Services in the basic training of personnel for Pay Accountancy and associated matters were designed to meet the needs of widely differing documentation, nomenclature and methods. To a great extent the methods used reflect the differing operational use which will be made of the Clerk. In the RN a Writer will go to a ship where he will be required to work with a minimum of supervision. The RM and Army Clerk may be employed in static offices or on detached duty with small units. The RAF Clerk almost always goes to a unit or to the RAF Personnel Management Centre, where supervision and advice are readily available. All the newly qualified 'Pay Clerks' are employed on pay accountancy matters and do comparable jobs for the initial 3-6 months of their employment following basic training. However, the single-Service documentation and procedures which they use are different and would not be understood by clerks from a different Service. Each Service uses a computer to assist in the computation of its pay, each of these computers at present only accepts single-Service inputs.

Conclusions

2. The DTCWP concluded that:

(a) whilst the three principal Services, individually, have accountancy computers which will accept only inputs and provide outputs of a single-Service nature, there is a continuing requirement for single-Service basic training;

(b) there is some degree of similarity in the initial employment of 'Pay Clerks' following basic training, but the documentation and procedures vary considerably between the Services;

(c) no Service has a guaranteed surplus capacity in the long term to accept the total requirement of another Service's basic training;

(d) where a single-Service is able to rationalize the employment of Clerks by merging trades or combining duties etc. this in itself will help to reduce training costs.

Recommendations

3. The DTCWP recommend that:

(a) no further investigation of the rationalization of basic training of the three principal Services 'Pay Clerks' should be made until there is common pay accountancy documentation and the introduction of a computer, or computers, which can accept inputs from and produce outputs to any Service;

Views of the Defence Training Committee (DTC)

4. In its original deliberations the DTC took note of the statement of the DTCWP that the existence of single Service computers was an obstacle towards rationalization. However, further investigation has shown that the existence of separate computers is not an insurmountable objection as the separate machines can be adapted, at a price, to accept all Service inputs and produce any required output. The real difficulty in rationalization of Pay Clerk training lies in the fact that terminology documentation, and administrative procedures differ widely between the Services. The DTC decided, that until the Services are in a position to introduce common procedures, unification of the training of pay clerks is not feasible.

APPENDIX 6 TO ANNEX A TO SCOE/31/9/2/5

CLERICAL STAFF

Introduction

1. In the RN, Writers are trained to carry out both pay and general office work. This is necessary because the ships in which the Writers are borne have insufficient space for men to perform pay and clerical duties separately. In the RM, whilst specialisation training is undertaken at Corporal level, general clerical duties may be undertaken by both Clerks (Pay and Records) and Clerks (Quartermaster). Both the Army and the RAF train and employ personnel for general clerical duties, including personnel and records administration, as distinct from pay duties.

Objectives

2. The objectives of the individual Service courses are as follows:

(a) *RN.* To enable the Writer to type up to 25 words per minute, process Service correspondence, make entries on personnel records run a small pay office, and assist in the preparation of cash accounts. RM Clerks (PR) are expected to undertake similar duties and deal with RM records which are run on a different system to those of the RN and the other Services.

(b) *Army.* To train Clerks to perform general clerical duties and to type up to 15 words per minute.

(c) *RAF.* To produce a fully skilled tradesman to perform general office clerical duties and to type at 25 words per minute.

3. The DTCWP found that many of the considerations which apply to Pay Clerks also applied to personnel employed on Clerical duties ; the present style of administration, procedures, and documentation of the single Services are necessarily diverse and there would appear to be insurmountable problems in bringing together the basic training of clerical staff.

Conclusions

4. The DTCWP concluded that :

(a) there is little scope for rationalisation of the basic clerical training because of the different single-Service regulations, personnel documentation, and clerical procedures ;

(b) no single-Service establishment has the forecast spare capacity to cater for all the Services basic clerical training ;

(c) the Army has a programmed instruction method of training their Clerks which has proved to be a successful and economical system.

Recommendations

5. The DTCWP recommended that :

(a) no further investigation into the rationalisation of the basic training of Services' Clerks should be made as this would not be feasible whilst the Services' regulations, personnel records, and general administration are organised on a single Service basis ;

(b) the programmed instruction system of teaching used by the Army should be considered by the other Services when Clerical training methods are being reviewed.

Views of the Defence Training Committee (DTC)

6. The DTC accepted the conclusions and recommendations of the Working Party, that at present procedures, documentation, and style of administration are so different in the separate Services that common training of Clerical Staff could not be sensibly introduced. The DTC decided that :

(a) There is no scope for co-location of training because of differing clerical procedures designed to meet different Service requirements.

(b) The RN, RM and RAF be invited to consider the Army's programmed learning methods.

APPENDIX 7 TO ANNEX A TO SCOE/31/9/2/5

DRIVERS

Method

1. Drivers are trained on formal courses which include classroom work, and practical driving. The Royal Marines train the great majority of their light vehicle (LV) drivers on courses held in units of Commando Forces RM under the instruction of Unit MT NCOs. A few are trained at RM Poole. Basic HGV courses lasting 7 weeks, and HGV conversion courses for those already qualified as LV drivers, are held at RM Poole.

2. Army drivers are taught throughout the Army at unit level; some as specialist drivers, some as part of another specialization. The DTCWP selected, as a typical centralized driver training establishment, 12 Driver Training Regt RCT, which conducts a course[1] for non-drivers through to HGV standard and also trains other personnel, including RAF Regiment, in tactical driving.

3. The Royal Air Force trains its drivers in two phases, LV and HGV. The LV phase averages 18 days[1]; the HGV phase is also self-pacing and lasts 2–3 weeks. The RAF also trains about 280 RN and 300 Army drivers each year.

Objectives

4. The objective of all basic training is to get the potential driver through the DOE Part 2 basic test. This, however, is only a partial goal, because the RM require their drivers to reach HGV, drive with trailers, cross country, in convoy, into and out of landing craft, and waterproof and camouflage vehicles. The Army (RCT) require all its drivers to reach HGV standard, to understand tactical driving, convoy work, and special load procedures. In addition there are 47 driver specialisations through the Army. The RAF normally trains to LV standard and converts the HGV standard after about 4 months experience. Its drivers often have to be able to drive on airfields and tow aircraft.

Location

5. The RM trains some of its drivers at RM Poole; this school could not accept trainees from other Services as it is fully committed. The Army trains over 2,000 drivers each year at Aldershot, but in addition about 2,500 soldiers are taught to drive each year in other Units. The RAF trains about 5,500 drivers including 280 RN and 300 Army at St Athan. All these schools are fully committed and could not accept an addition to their task; the environmental effect of concentrating the training of all drivers in one location would also need careful study; protests from local residents would be likely.

Conclusions

6. The DTCWP concluded that:

(a) Over 10,000 Servicemen and women receive basic driver training annually, about half of these are trained at 2 main centres, Aldershot and St Athan. The numbers involved are so large that to concentrate all training in one existing centre would be impossible for reasons of accommodation and support services, and any significant increase in the number of Service vehicles used for driver training in either location would have an adverse effect on local traffic densities.

(b) Where possible joint training is already being carried out;

(1) The RAF train 280 RN and 300 drivers annually.

(2) The Army train personnel of other Services on an opportunity basis when vacancies are available.

(3) The Army train RAF Regiment drivers in tactical driving.

(4) Joint Service conversion courses for HGV drivers are starting in January 1974[2].

(c) Different methods of training with varying course lengths and content are justified by the individual Services requirement to train a driver for a particular type of operation or non-operational role.

(d) No viable alternative exists to the present system whereby a substantial part of driver training is concentrated at Aldershot and St Athan, and for the rest the Services train their own drivers at Unit level.

---

[1] Neither of these courses are of fixed length. Trainees join continually and are given as much or as little instruction as they need, leaving when considered qualified; this is known as the ' self-pacing ' method.

[2] The courses started on 1st January, 1974.

Recommendations

7. The Working Party recommended that:

(*a*) Joint Service co-operation in all forms of driver training which already exists should continue.

(*b*) Further rationalisation and/or amalgamation of certain Service driver training is not practicable and should not be pursued.

View of the Defence Training Committee (DTC)

8. The DTC took note that the annual task amounted to about 10,000 personnel receiving driving training each year and that one half of these are trained at two centres, the remainder at Unit level throughout the UK. To concentrate this entire effort in one place would have an adverse effect on the area chosen, and since many driving instructors are locally employed civilians, recruiting of sufficient numbers would be an exceptional problem. Joint training already partially takes place where possible, but different methods of training are used in the Service where a driver is eventually going on to a different type of employment.

9. The DTC decided that:

(*a*) Where Joint Service co-operation already exists it should continue.

(*b*) Further amalgamation is not necessary, and is environmentally undesirable.

(*c*) Where different teaching methods are used, and these are geared to the eventual role of the driver, they should continue to be used.

APPENDIX 8 TO ANNEX A TO SCOE/31/9/2/5

EDUCATION OFFICERS

Introduction

1. The DTCWP found that a tri-Service Working Group was studying the initial training of Education Officers simultaneously, therefore, to avoid duplication the DTCWP studied their deliberations and conclusions.

Method

2. The DTCWP found that first training of Education Officers is not basic training as the embryonic Education Officer has been trained by the Universities, the Colleges of Education, and other higher educational establishments which produce graduates, graduate equivalents, and trained teachers. The particular mix of qualifications required and the training given in the 3 Services depends on the roles which the Education Officer will play in each of the Services.

Objectives

3. In the RN the majority of Instructor Officers are employed in technical training; they provide instruction in the educational, technical and operational parts of Naval courses from elementary work to degree and post-graduate level studies. The professional training gives an introduction to the Naval training, and teaching methods in the Naval environment of ship management and operations at sea.

4. The Royal Army Educational Corps officer is employed in adult or junior training units or Army Education Centres. The professional training gives primary emphasis to the details of the educational requirements of the syllabi of the Army's " functionally based " Education Promotion System which is a method whereby the Army no longer teaches education as an extension of general education as taught in schools. Instead of English the Army teaches communication skills, report writing, service letter writing etc; instead of arithmetic military calculations are taught. At a later stage in his career the RAEC officer is involved in higher voluntary education.

5. The Royal Air Force Education Officer is employed in teaching the educational component of flying and technical training, with the preparation of airmen for promotion both educationally and in trade proficiency, and providing voluntary general education.

6. The aim of all courses is to teach the Education Officers of the 3 Services the special professional skills and Service procedures to enable them to carry out their duties in the different roles in the 3 Services.

Recommendations

7. The DTCWP recommended that:

    (a) It is neither reasonable nor economic to institute joint professional training of Service Education Officers.

Views of the Defence Training Committee (DTC)

8. The DTC took note that the basic training of Education Officers was provided by civilian educational establishments, and that the initial professional training given to officers was designed to orientate them to the different jobs they would do in each of the 3 Services, and the necessarily different methods used in discharging their tasks.

9. The DTC decided that:

    (a) There is no scope for the amalgamation of the initial professional training given to education officers because the objectives of each service differs.

APPENDIX 9 TO ANNEX A TO SCOE/31/9/2/5

SERVICE POSTAL PERSONNEL

Introduction

1. The DTCWPs investigation showed that Service mail in transit is handled by either the National Post Organisation or the Postal, Courier and Communications Branch of the Royal Engineers (PCC) (RE). This branch of the Royal Engineers provides a service for the processing of overseas classified and unclassified official and private mails for the Royal Navy, the Army, the Royal Air Force, their families and associated organisations. It also provides a postal service to Royal Navy vessels in home waters and visiting warships.

Training

2. Soldiers from the Royal Engineers are trained on a basic course of 7 weeks duration at the Home Postal Courier and Communications Depot in London; a number of WRAC women are also trained in postal duties.

3. In the RN, postal orderly training is included in the basic course for Leading Patrolman in the regulating branch, other RMs and Ratings required for Postal Orderly duties are given 2-day familiarisation courses. The Army also run 2–3 day courses in individual Commands for Soldiers detailed to be Unit Postal Orderlies. The Royal Air Force has a very small training task to provide pre-employment training (primarily in handling/control of money) for clerks who are to be employed in the few unit post offices not manned by the GPO. The course lasts one week.

Conclusions

4. The DTCWP concluded that the postal services provided by the Postal, Courier and Communications Branch of the Royal Engineers meets the Services' requirements.

Recommendations

5. The DTCWP recommended that there is no need to rationalise further the training of personnel engaged on postal duties in the Services.

Views of the Defence Training Committee (DTC)

6. The DTC agreed with the Working Party that rationalisation of postal services was as complete as possible, and decided that;

(*a*) the service provided by the RE (PCC) met the Service requirements;

(*b*) the very short courses run in the single-Services for local Postal Orderlies were necessary for the security of official and private mails.

(*c*) no further rationalisation was possible.

APPENDIX 10 TO ANNEX A TO SCOE/31/9/2/5

PHYSICAL TRAINING INSTRUCTORS

Method

1. Members of the Seaman Branch of the RN are trained on a formal 22-week course which qualified them as an Instructor in the rank of Leading Seaman. The Royal Marine PTI is a General Duties NCO drawn from mature trained men. These trainees, who will have already passed a Junior Command Course, are given 16-weeks formal training becoming Instructors in the rank of Corporal. Army PTIs may become members of the Army Physical Training Corps through three stages of training:

(*a*) mature soldiers of all arms at the rank of Lance Corporal or above are given a 9-week course to qualify as Assistant Instructors;

(*b*) after about 2 years, approximately 15 per cent of Assistant Instructors are accepted for further training of 13 weeks to qualify as Advanced Instructors: both these categories remain regimental soldiers;

(*c*) at a later stage about 5 per cent of Advanced Instructors are given a further 22-week course to qualify them for transfer to the Army Physical Training Corps.

2. The RAF PTI is mainly recruited direct from civilian life; he is given 4 weeks elementary parachute training and a 23-week trade training course qualifying him for the rank of Corporal. At a later stage suitable PTIs are selected for training as Parachute Jumping Instructors because the Physical Education Branch of the RAF is responsible for parachute training.

Objectives

3. The DTCWP reported the objectives of the Services as follows:

(*a*) *RN*

Naval PTIs are required to have a high level of fitness, a knowledge of recreational administration and management, together with instructional and coaching ability.

(*b*) *RM*

The RM PTIs task is to develop battle physical fitness, as well as to coach trainees, officiate at sports and to assist in Unit sports administration.

(*c*) *Army*

Army Instructors retain their regimental identities and employ their physical training skills to supplement their basic military duties. They are required to assist in maintaining the mandatory levels of fitness within the Army to enhance the combat readiness of the soldier.

(*d*) *RAF*

The RAF PTI is required to have a good level of physical fitness as a complementary attribute to the principles of teaching and the methods of administering and supervising recreational activities at station level.

Locations

4. The RN train its personnel at HMS TEMERAIRE, Portsmouth. As a consequence of Hampshire County Council development plans it will be necessary to move these facilities from their present site. Planning for this is well advanced.

5. The Royal Marines train their PTIs at the Physical Training Wing, Deal, but this Wing may possibly move to Lympstone in the late 1970s. Co-location with the RN school was considered in 1971 but it was recommended a further study should be made after the move of the RN school.

6. The Army School of PT is at Aldershot and a decision will be taken in late 1974 whether or not to embark on a major modernisation plan in 1979–80.

7. Royal Air Force training takes place at St Athan and is expected to remain there although training methods are under scrutiny and may be revised.

Conclusions

8. The DTCWP concluded that:

(a) the Services have different training objectives and career structures that preclude joint Service basic training whilst the objectives remain in their present form. However, the differences between the present training courses for Physical Training Instructors would not constitute an insuperable objection to the co-location of the schools of Physical Training Instruction in the same establishment (provided this were at a place which would permit the individual Services to maintain their responsibilities for Service sport if co-location seemed desirable and was likely to be economical).

(b) Consideration should be given to the co-location of 2 or more PT Schools, whenever there is a requirement for an existing school to be moved into new purpose-built accommodation.

(c) The competitive and physical elements of joint Service rivalry are well served by single-Service Physical Training Instructors training and that spirit of competition between the Services is good for morale and recruiting.

Recommendations

9. The DTCWP recommended that:

(a) the single-Service methods of training Physical Training Instructors should be retained whilst the training objectives are dis-similar.

(b) co-location of basic Physical Training Instructor training for 2 or more Services should be considered if ever there is a future requirement to re-locate single-Service training into new purpose-built accommodation.

Views of the Defence Training Committee (DTC)

10. The DTC thought that cogent arguments could be put forward for a joint Service training of basic Physical Training Instructors; it was thought that single-Service training objectives were not too dis-similar. At present accommodation is a problem because none of the present schools could cope with all Services requirements and a new-build would be extremely costly. It was pointed out that both the RN and Army were at the briefing stage on new-built accommodation and would be disappointed at any delay.

11. The DTC decided that the RAF would:

(a) co-ordinate the views of the three Services on the desirability of joint Service PT Instructor training;

(b) ascertain the state of building plans on new PT Instructor accommodation in the three Services;

(c) produce a paper on (a) and (b) above to the DTC including the recommendations.

12. The results of this study are expected to be available late in 1974.

Printed in England by Her Majesty's Stationery Office at St Stephen's Parliamentary Press
399477 Dd. 252621 K14 3/75
ISBN 0 10 022205 6